D1244646

More Difficult Sayings of Jesus

More Difficult Sayings of Jesus

WILLIAM NEIL
and
STEPHEN H. TRAVIS

MOWBRAY
LONDON & OXFORD

Copyright © William Neil 1979 and Stephen H. Travis
1981

ISBN 0 264 66552 X

First published 1981
by A. R. Mowbray & Co. Ltd
Saint Thomas House, Becket Street
Oxford, OX1 1SJ

Photoset in Great Britain by
REDWOOD BURN LIMITED
Trowbridge, Wiltshire
Printed in Great Britain by Richard Clay
(The Chaucer Press) Bungay, Suffolk

ISBN 0-264-66552-X

Biblical quotations are from the
New English Bible, unless otherwise indicated.

Foreword

When he died in November 1979, William Neil left the half-completed typescript of this book. It was to be a follow-up to *What Jesus Really Meant*, a study of difficult sayings of Jesus which had been widely welcomed when it appeared in 1975. When the publishers invited me to complete the book by adding a further sixteen chapters to those which Dr Neil had already written, I was more than ready to do so. For I had met him occasionally through my association with Nottingham University, where he was Warden of Hugh Stewart Hall and Reader in Biblical Studies. And I had long admired his skill in communicating the message of the Bible and the fruits of biblical study to ordinary people. With William Barclay and A. M. Hunter, he was part of that Scottish trinity of distinguished scholars who for the last thirty years have made the Bible both exciting and intelligible to multitudes in the English-speaking world.

It is fitting, then, that William Neil's last book should be one in which he sheds light on difficult sayings of Jesus and explains their meaning for today. And he would have sent it forth, as he did his *One Volume Bible Commentary*, with the comment: 'Unless all that is written about the Bible is an inducement to the reader to turn to the Bible itself it is largely misdirected effort.'

I have tried to make my own chapters similar to Dr Neil's in their general approach, but without slavish imitation. The result, I trust, is a book which helps to fulfil his great hope, that readers should understand – and follow – the message of Jesus.

St John's College, Nottingham   Stephen Travis
May, 1981

Contents

PART ONE

1

How blest are the sorrowful; they shall find consolation.
MATTHEW 5.4

The blessings of suffering

The Beatitudes which come at the beginning of the Sermon on the Mount in chapter 5 of St Matthew's Gospel present us with an arresting series of paradoxes. They describe the character of those who place themselves under the rule of God, who commit themselves to be fully obedient to his will – and a strange picture they present. All their attributes are the direct opposite of ordinary secular values. They are the humble of spirit, the merciful, the pure in heart, the peacemakers. But these, says Jesus, are the people who are truly blest. Perhaps the most unlikely group to be called 'blest' are the 'sorrowful'. Yet there is no escaping the claim of Jesus that the truly happy folk are those who know what sorrow and suffering means. This is difficult teaching indeed!

I visited a sweet old lady in hospital who knew as well as I did that she would never rise from her sick-bed again, and, as I left, her parting words were a quotation from Psalm 55 verse 19 in the King James Version: 'Because they have no changes, therefore they fear not God.' She knew what it meant to be changed from being an active and sprightly young woman to being a poor crippled old invalid, dependent on others to help her to meet the simplest demands of daily existence. She needed to be helped just to keep living. But she had learned to find that help by turning to God in prayer. She had found out through her suffering what the author of the letter to the Hebrews knew to be true when he wrote of Jesus: 'For since he himself has passed through the test of suffering, he is able to help those who are meeting their test now.' (Heb. 2.18)

F. W. Robertson in one of his sermons says this: 'Shut out suffering, and you see only one side of this strange and fearful thing, the life of man. Brightness and happiness and rest – that is not life. It is only one side of life. Christ saw both sides.' There is a popular saying: 'Never trouble trouble till trouble troubles you'. This is good sense. We need never go out of our way to look for sorrow. We all get our share. And none of us likes it when it comes our way. But what we can do, and ought to do, is to face up to it and learn from it. It may be illness or bereavement in the family. It may be disappointed ambition, a broken marriage, financial disaster or a dead-end job. And let us not forget that the hardships and sorrows of others are our opportunity.

That depressing Old Testament writer Ecclesiastes, who kept finding that everything was emptiness and vanity, would have come to a different conclusion if he had not been so wrapped up in his own pleasures. We do not know anything about him except what he tells us in his short book. He seems to have been an elderly well-to-do citizen of Jerusalem who had pulled out all the stops to find happiness. He had tried the old recipes of wine, women and song, and had added to these literature and the collection of *objets d'art*. But they all turned to ashes in his mouth. He had to confess failure. 'Vanity of vanities, all is vanity'. The one thing he does not seem to have tried was helping his neighbour, forgetting himself and thinking of others.

For this is surely the sovereign cure for introspection and self-pity – to take upon our own shoulders part of the world's suffering. We are not called on to find answers to the gigantic problems which defeat statesmen and drive men and women of goodwill close to despair. But we can look around for the minor casualties of life in our own small circle of experience, where what is needed is not dramatic solutions but just a hand of friendship and a word of sympathy. So long as these are not merely empty gestures but meaningful outreaches from the heart we are sharing in the great mass of the sorrows of mankind. And it is a costly business. Every act of self sacrifice where we put the needs of others before our own seems to be a loss to ourselves but it is in a truer sense an enrichment, and, more important, it is what God requires of us.

If it were left to ourselves to run the world in the way we would like it, we should no doubt try to eliminate all the sharp edges and rough passages of our day to day experience. Of course we must strive to banish injustice, improve the lot of the underprivileged, seek to rescue life's casualties and raise the standards of health and education. But God seems to have constructed the world in such a way that we give of our best when we are kept on our toes. We need to be challenged and prodded into action in order to become fully human. Pastor Niemöller has said: 'Jesus Christ is human, we are not.' And how did Jesus attain his perfect humanity? Not by living a feather-bedded existence but by confronting hardship, opposition and the total vileness of human nature. He was above all men, 'a man of sorrows and acquainted with grief'.

We must try, however, to follow in his footsteps. And if we do that we cannot ignore the pain and suffering that surrounds us and the cry of those who need our help and comfort and sympathy. Jesus has often been called, 'a man for others,' but he was first of all 'a man for God'. It was his total commitment to God which led him to love his neighbours, but also enabled him to face victoriously the tragic side of his own experience of life.

These fine words of Robert Browning Hamilton are worth remembering:

I walked a mile with Pleasure
She chattered all the way,
But left me none the wiser
For all she had to say.

I walked a mile with Sorrow,
And ne'er a word said she,
But oh, the things I learned from her
When Sorrow walked with me!

(quoted in *The Challenge of New Testament Ethics*,
L. H. Marshall, p. 80)

2

You are salt to the world ... You are light for all the world.   MATTHEW 5.13, 14

The salt of the earth

The more familiar form of these sayings of Jesus is to be found in the older translations: 'you are the salt of the earth ... you are the light of the world.' In either case our immediate response would be to say: Not true! It may have been true of the disciples to whom Jesus was speaking in the Sermon on the Mount but it is certainly not true of us ordinary Christians today. How could we, looking round the average congregation in the churches to which we belong have the effrontery to claim that we are like the salt that makes tasteless food appetising by giving savour to the life of the community we live in, or by shining out as bright lights which illuminate the greyness of a drab and bewildered world?

But of course when we look more closely at those words of Jesus in their context it is quite obvious that he was neither praising the disciples nor giving his present day followers a pat on the back. He was challenging and encouraging his earliest disciples – and us today – to fill the role of salt and light in bringing out the best flavour in the life of our society and in dispelling the gloom of a sombre world. Lesslie Newbigin has described the Christian as 'one who has forever given up the hope of being able to think of himself as a good man'. But the Christian is at the same time one who has *never* given up the hope of being able to help, in however small a way,

7

in God's work of transforming the chaos and confusion into which man's sin and folly have led him.

There is little enough that most of us can do to improve the political flavour of the world except to cast our votes when opportunity arises in a responsible way and in accordance with what our conscience tells us. But here we are at once in difficulty, for one man's conscience tells him the exact opposite of what another man's conscience compels him to do. We must recognise that with the best will in the world we can never be sure that we are right. This is why we must question the confident assertion of Albert Camus who avers: 'what the world expects of Christians is that they should speak out, loud and clear, and that they should voice their condemnation in such a way that never a doubt, never the slightest doubt could arise in the heart of the simplest man'. Maybe this is what the world expects of us, but except in a very limited field this is just what we cannot do.

Obviously Christians must condemn wanton cruelty to men or animals, child neglect, indifference to suffering, disregard of the plight of the aged and unwanted. But there is nothing specifically Christian in this. Ordinary humanity would compel atheists and agnostics to react in the same way. Most of the issues on which we are called to make decisions one way or the other are nothing like so clear cut. Christians can easily condemn war as wasteful, inhuman and in the long run futile. But how do we achieve peace? There are as many pros as cons in any proffered solution, and Christians are no more gifted with ready answers to this and the other great problems of modern life than Muslims, Hindus or Communists.

How then can we become the 'salt' and 'light' that our Lord expects us to be? Dietrich Bonhoeffer in his *Letters and Papers from Prison* points us towards an answer. 'To be a Christian does not mean to be religious in a particular way, to cultivate some particular form of asceticism (as a sinner, a penitent, or a saint) but to be a man. It is not some religious act that makes a Christian what he is, but participation in the suffering of God in the life of the world. It is only by living completely in this world that one learns to believe. One must abandon every attempt to make something of oneself, whether it be a saint, a converted sinner, a churchman, a righteous man or an unrighteous one, a sick man or a healthy one. This is what I mean by worldliness – taking life in one's stride, with all its duties and problems, its successes and failures, its experiences and helplessness.'

'Taking life in one's stride' without pretence or posing seems to be as good a recipe for becoming 'salt' and 'light' in the community as we shall find. There is nothing dramatic or particularly heroic about it, but then most of us are not the stuff that heroes are made of or candidates for major roles on the stage of life. There are two sides to taking life in our stride, according to Bonhoeffer. One side of it is concerned with our successes and failures. If we are to be 'salt' and 'light' in our community we must be seen as people who are not over elated by success or unduly depressed by failure. Christians should be known for their stability of character, for their equable temper, and for their cheerful disposition. In our younger days if we were in the Boy Scouts – and presumably comparable youth organisations would have similar good counsel to give their members – we were told that a Scout sings and whistles under all difficulties. Perhaps that is too much to expect of us in middle age or even more advanced years – especially if nature has cast us in a sombre mould – but we can at least present a calm and unflurried front to the world and refuse to be carried away by our little successes or plunged into gloom by our failures.

But there is also the other side. Life has its duties and problems. And here a Christian can best fulfil the Lord's command to be 'salt' and 'light' by being the sort of person who can be trusted to keep his word, to be

strictly honest where money is concerned, to be generous and charitable in our dealings with others, and not
to judge our neighbours harshly but always to give them
the benefit of the doubt. As for the problems of life,
they are as many and varied as there are men and
women alive. As Christians all we can do is to set an
example by tackling them bravely with God's help and
guidance.

3

You have a rich reward in heaven.

MATTHEW 5.12

Pie in the sky

Jesus is speaking here in the Sermon on the Mount of those who suffer insults and persecution for his sake. He assures his followers not only that they are 'blest' when this happens to them, and urges them to accept such treatment gladly, but also promises them that they will be richly rewarded in the life hereafter. This promise of receiving a reward in heaven to compensate for ill-treatment on earth is a new element in biblical teaching which we owe to Jesus. In this same verse he mentions the Old Testament prophets as having endured the same persecution as Christians might expect, but for them there was no question of counting on a rich reward in heaven since in Old Testament times there was no clear cut belief in an after life at all. For Jesus, however, nothing was more certain and after the Resurrection his followers cherished his words: 'There are many dwelling places in my Father's house; if it were not so I should have told you; for I am going there on purpose to prepare a place for you'. (John 14.2) But they had also to take seriously his words on a different occasion which spoke of the other kind of after life and meant ultimate separation from God. (Mark 9.42–48)

Many people have felt that the whole idea of rewards and punishments hereafter for good or bad behaviour in this life is unworthy of Christianity. Joe Hill has expressed this in memorable and amusing terms 'You'll get pie in the sky when you die.' (*Folk Songs of North America*) Others have been less amusing and more bitter in their criticism of any religion which encourages its followers to live nobly and virtuously because it will pay them in the long run, and hold up for our admiration those who mould their lives on duty which they generally regard in Wordsworth's phrase as the 'Stern Daughter of the Voice of God.'

The writers of the book of Proverbs in the Old Testament have no doubt that to serve God a man must live a good life. Just as they have no doubt that if he does live a good life he will get his reward in this world and vice versa. It is this belief that goodness is a paying proposition that gives the book of Proverbs its characteristically utilitarian and prudential cast. The sensible man is the man who does what is right. The fool is the man who does what is wrong, not so much from the point of view of the wrongness of the act but because evil-doing is invariably followed by retribution. So long as this was taken by and large, it was true enough as a philosophy of history for a nation or a community. But in the short span of a man's life it must have occurred to the authors of this prudential morality that goodness is not always rewarded by prosperity and evil by misfortune. The way out was of course to say that if an apparently good man suffered it must be on account of the sins of his fathers or on account of some secret sins of his own. This rather unsatisfactory solution was questioned by the author of the book of Job. He depicted Job as the unhappy victim of intolerable suffering who nevertheless maintained his innocence of serious misdemeanours against the adverse judgment of the whole community, even against God himself. But in his epilogue to the book the author had to bow to the pulic opinion of his times, compensating Job for his afflictions by restoring his fortunes and giving him twice as much as he had before. (Job 42.10)

Was this what Jesus meant when he spoke of 'a rich reward in heaven'? Was he offering inducements to good behaviour, generous acts, works of charity and mercy by holding out the promise of compensations in the after life, or conversely by threatening punishment beyond death for failure to live the good life here and now? L. H. Marshall rightly says 'the idea of performing a good deed for the sake of a material reward is ignoble and reduces virtue to the mean posture of accepting gratuities'.* He cites the cases of Joan of Arc and Garibaldi as winning our admiration rather for the very fact that they refused any reward for their great services to the people of their time. For Joan, when offered by the Dauphin anything she asked for, simply requested that the poor people of her native village of Domremy should have their taxes remitted, and Garibaldi, declining King Victor Emmanuel's tempting offers of titles and wealth for his family and a royal castle for himself, accepted merely a bag of seed-corn for his island farm.

Surely Jesus would have approved the choices of both St Joan and Garibaldi. The 'rich reward in heaven' of which he spoke was not in any sense a material reward. But there is, and there must be, a reward for a life of good works, otherwise Christianity would not make sense. The reward is, however, not to be measured in commercial terms but in terms of inward satisfaction, peace of mind and a clear conscience – all of them more real and more enduring than any financial gain. And there is nothing wrong in looking for that kind of reward. On the contrary, if this is God's world, the men and women who live their lives in accordance with Bible teaching and the example of Christ and the saints are in tune with the mind and purpose which created and control the universe. Any action which is in harmony with God's will is therefore bound to be rewarded.

Moreover, although the New Testament says rela-

* *The Challenge of New Testament Ethics* p. 202

tively little about life after death and does not encourage us to speculate on what it will be like, it affirms and proclaims it from beginning to end. In St Paul's words, now we see only puzzling reflections in a mirror and our knowledge is only partial. (1 Cor. 13.12) But what we can glimpse of God here and what we can sense of his presence now encourage us to hope for fuller understanding and deeper experience hereafter. Then Jesus' words about 'a rich reward in heaven' will become reality in the life which is eternal.

4

Look at him! a glutton and a drinker.

MATTHEW 11.19

Asceticism

These words do not constitute a difficult saying of Jesus. Here our Lord is simply repeating what was apparently a common description of him by the 'good' people of his day. It tells us more about them than about Jesus. We all know the gossip that flies around every small town and village in any country. Woe betide the man who is seen going into the bar of a hotel or a public house! He is immediately dubbed a drunkard by all the total abstainers in the community. Allowing for the difference in time and place it must have been much the same in Galilee. But in the case of Jesus there was the special problem that he was supposed to be a 'holy' man, a rabbi, a prophet, but he was not behaving like one.

John the Baptist, on the other hand, had lived up to the popular idea of what a 'holy' man should be like. He had dressed like an Old Testament prophet in a rough coat of camel's hair fastened with a leather belt; he had existed on the sparse food of the desert – locusts and wild honey. (Matt. 3.4) Jesus, however, had done nothing like that, but had eaten the normal food of the Galilean peasants with whom he mixed and in a wine-drinking country had taken his share of the ordinary table wine. He likewise gave offence to his self-righteous critics by mixing with the wrong sort of company on social occasions. (Mark 2.15)

Some people have always found it difficult to draw the line between self-indulgence and mortification of the flesh. Neither of these should form part of Christian behaviour. It is easy to see why eating or drinking to excess is physically and spiritually harmful to us but it is not always so obvious that excessive fasting or ill-treatment of our bodies is equally foreign to the spirit and example of Jesus. In the early days of the Church the monks and hermits who fled to the desert to escape the temptations of civilisation, living on top of pillars, scourging themselves frequently, existing on bread and water, denying themselves not only luxuries but the bare necessities of life, acquired a reputation for holiness by such practices which was both spurious and totally misleading.

The general impression we get in the gospels of the day-to-day behaviour of Jesus is one of a completely normal and very human man. His healing and teaching ministry was inspired and empowered by frequent and prolonged spells of solitary communion with God; from these he drew his strength. But in other respects he has left us an example of one who loved to mix with his fellow men, who enjoyed the beauty of God's good earth, who was fond of children, who was a welcome guest at a marriage feast, and who indeed likened his companionship with his disciples to the gaiety of a wedding celebration. As E. F. Scott declared roundly, 'With the ascetic ideal he had no sympathy' and in keeping with this the first Christians got on with their jobs, whatever they happened to be, and made their work the channel through which they expressed their new-found faith.

Jesus himself never married although he taught that marriage was the normal man-woman relationship. As he explained to his disciples, some renounce marriage 'for the sake of the kingdom of Heaven' (Matt. 19.12) and many clergy and missionaries in the work of the Church throughout the centuries have chosen celibacy because they believed that thereby they could more effectively devote their lives to the service of God, without the complications and responsibilities of family commitments. But as St Paul tells us (I Cor. 9.5) the first disciples and Jesus' own brothers felt themselves bound by no such obligations, and were accompanied by their wives on their various assignments.

'A glutton and a drinker!' What a revolting description of anybody! Yet this was what the narrow-minded religious authorities had to say of our Lord. It simply shows us how wickedly wrong we can be when we apply our petty little tape measures to the man next-door, to Mr X down the street, or to the vast number of decent ordinary Christian people who 'like a drink', enjoy a smoke, in short, who in these respects are no different from people who would not call themselves 'Christians' at all.

Well, then, are Christians not distinguishable from others? Of course they are! But they should be distinguishable by their *positive* contribution to society, not by their *negative* witness. Let us come back to Jesus. Although his critics accused him of being a 'glutton and a drinker' this was not the opinion of his followers or of the crowds of ordinary folk who flocked to hear him. They thought of him as Master, Teacher, Healer – one who brought comfort and hope and encouragement to sad and lonely folk, who opened men's eyes to the beauty of God's creation, who made them aware of the goodness that lurks in unexpected places, and taught them to see the hand of God even in adversity.

At the end of World War 2 in Italy where I had been an army chaplain, we ran a 'School of Christian Leadership' at Assisi, which was not intended to create leaders but to show those who attended our courses, and had already shown their qualities of leadership in the army, that Christian leadership was the best kind of leadership. We chaplains, five of us, took about thirty men at a time, living under the same roof for a fortnight and giving lectures, organising discussions, answering questions and visiting the places that had been associated with St Francis, whose spirit still hovered over the town and surrounding countryside. The courses were voted by the troops to have been a great success; but we had the greatest difficulty in persuading regimental commanders and sergeant-majors that the kind of men we wanted for these courses was not the goody-goody type who never missed a religious service and even organised prayer meetings on their own. We wanted – and soon got – normal healthy young officers and NCOs who had already proved their mettle in the rough and tumble of army life. It was these 'gluttons and drinkers', as the Pharisees – ancient and modern – would have dubbed them, who won the war for us. Thank God for them all!

5

Who do you say I am?

Who was Jesus?

Jesus had a disconcerting habit of asking uncomfortable questions, but perhaps none were quite so searching and vital as this – vital for himself and even more so for us. The place was a country road near Caesarea Philippi, north of Galilee, and the time was about half way through his short public ministry. On the day of his baptism in the river Jordan at the hands of John the Baptist Jesus had had a vision of heaven and had heard in his heart the words of God 'Thou art my Son, my Beloved'. For him it had been confirmation of his growing recognition, during the 'hidden years' of his obscure life in the carpenter's shop at Nazareth, that his relationship to God was of an intimacy which was not shared by those around him, and, as we may guess, that his growing sense of power which was soon to be demonstrated in healings, exorcisms, and even more dramatic ways, was unique. There was no other way to describe it.

But who was he? The religious authorities of the time had no hesitation in denouncing him as an imposter – a charlatan and a law-breaker. The crowds who flocked round him acclaimed him as a 'wonder-worker' – a magician. Neither of these was the answer Jesus wanted. But what answer would his disciples give? These were the men who had been closest to him – who had seen him in public and in private, who had heard his teaching, watched him confront and discomfit the religious experts of the day with an authority that they claimed but clearly did not possess. His followers had seen him heal broken bodies and calm deranged minds. Even more mysterious had been his power over the natural world in stilling a storm on the Lake of Galilee so that they had asked each other, filled with awe, 'Who can this be? Even the wind and sea obey him.' (Mark 4.41)

It would seem that Jesus had let all these experiences sink into the minds of his companions but had not until now challenged them to give him the answer he was seeking, the answer that would confirm what from the day of his baptism he had known to be the truth about himself. He began by asking them what was the verdict of the crowds who had flocked to hear and see him in Galilee. They replied that some thought of him as John the Baptist come back to life, after having been so cruelly done to death by King Herod in fulfilment of a drunken promise. (Mark 6. 17–28) Others again claimed that Jesus was Elijah who, according to Old Testament expectation, would one day reappear to deliver and restore Israel. (Mal. 4. 5–6) Or some thought that Jesus was the reincarnation of one or other of the prophets.

But when Jesus asked the disciples the straight question: But who do *you* say I am? it was Peter, impulsive as ever, who put his finger on the answer Jesus wanted. 'You are the Messiah'. Peter, who stood foremost in our Lord's regard as the rock on which he would build his Church, intuitively on this occasion spoke for all the others. But it is in Matthew's gospel that the veil is lifted from Jesus' own thoughts and we are shown that he regarded Peter's confession of faith as a God-given revelation. (Matt. 16. 13–20)

Yet the strange paradox is that having elicited the answer he wanted, that he was the long awaited Messiah and the fulfilment of all the hopes of his people, Jesus now, as so often elsewhere in the gospel story, completely banned the use of the word Messiah relating to himself and chose instead the term Son of Man. The reason was plain. 'Messiah' over the years had come to have in the minds of ordinary people political and military overtones. The religious significance of the term – God's anointed – deliverer and liberator – had been lost and 'messiah' had come to be thought of as a new Judas Maccabaeus who would rid Israel of its Roman oppressors by force of arms. There were thousands of young Jews inside Palestine and far beyond who were merely waiting for the signal and who would rally to the cause of any likely patriot. This, however, was not at all how Jesus interpreted his messianic vocation. As Mark tells us, his response to Peter's confession was to unveil his own deepest convictions about himself and the role he had chosen for Israel's Messiah to follow – the way of Isaiah's suffering Servant (Isa. 53) which would lead to a cross.

If we can with all reverence and humility try to plumb the depths of Jesus' thoughts about himself, as reflected in the gospels, it would seem that his basic conviction was that of his close relationship to God which he saw as that of Father and Son. It recurs right through the first three gospels but is uniquely concentrated in the gospel of John. This is where indeed we stand upon 'holy ground', for mystery lies at the centre of the gospel message and we cannot side-step it. But the Fourth Gospel brings us closest to the heart of the matter. Jesus' words in his last great discourse (John 14–17) are the climax of the whole gospel story of God's intervention to save us from the consequences of our own failure and folly. Here are some of them – 'set your troubled hearts at rest. Trust in God always; trust also in me. There are many dwelling-places in my Father's house. . . . I am going there on purpose to prepare a place for you. . . . I am the way; I am the truth and I am life. . . . Anyone who has seen me has seen the

Father. . . . I am the vine, and you the branches. He who dwells in me, as I dwell in him, bears much fruit; for apart from me you can do nothing. . . . As the Father has loved me, so I have loved you. Dwell in my love. . . . There is no greater love than this, that a man should lay down his life for his friends. You are my friends, if you do what I command you.'

6

Away with you, Satan.

Short cuts rejected

This astonishing outburst on the part of Jesus was not, as we might have imagined, directed towards one of his enemies but towards his closest friend and staunchest supporter, the rock-like Peter. The occasion on which the words were spoken was equally astonishing. For it was immediately after Peter had with unerring insight given his Master the answer he had hoped for, and waited for, to his question about who he really was. (see chapter 5.) This, as Matthew's Gospel tells us, was an answer received by Jesus with wholehearted satisfaction as an inspired revelation. (Matt. 16. 13–20) Peter had said: You are the Messiah.

But almost immediately, as it would seem, the atmosphere changed. We find Jesus angrily denouncing his chief disciple for acting as the devil's advocate, calling him a 'stumbling-block', a 'hindrance' to his Master's purpose. What had happened? It was simply that with the best will in the world Peter was trying to save Jesus from himself and from what Peter regarded as Jesus' woeful misunderstanding of what it meant to be the Messiah. For Peter had just put into words what the whole company of Jesus' followers had increasingly come to recognise as the truth about their enigmatic Master, that he was no mere teacher, or prophet in the succession of Isaiah, Jeremiah and the whole galaxy of

Old Testament spokesmen for God, but the Lord's unique anointed representative on earth—the fulfilment of the hopes and prayers of Israel over the centuries. Messiah meant king, conqueror, and Jesus had accepted the title.

But to the concern and consternation of Peter, and no doubt of the other disciples as well, Jesus had at once not only forbidden them to call him Messiah openly; worse than that, he had begun to speak of his coming visit to Jerusalem as one that would end not in homage and acclamation but in suffering and death. This was too much for Peter and more than he could stand. Seizing Jesus by the arm he took him sharply to task. Suffering and death, we can almost hear him say, are no part of Messiah's destiny. You were born to conquer and rule Israel! Lead us against the Roman occupiers of our country and we shall be free!

The zealots, whom nowadays we should call nationalists or terrorists, had been saying this sort of thing for some time. One of them indeed had forsaken his revolutionary activities and had been admitted to the inner fellowship of the Twelve. (Mark 3.19) But there was deep political unrest in Israel in the time of Jesus and strong resentment against the Roman occupying power. Jesus consistently set his face against any involvement in popular anti-Roman feeling. We get a revealing insight into the tenseness of the local situation and an indication of the danger to which Jesus saw his mission exposed, in John 6.15, where we are told that there was strong pressure on him to force him to accept the office of Israel's messianic king. That he could have done this if he had wished there is no doubt. Thousands of young Jews, inside and outside Palestine, would have rallied to the standard of one whom they would have seen as a new Judas Maccabaeus, who had led Israel to independence two centuries before.

But this was not the way to the Messiahship that Jesus had in mind. Ever since his baptism in the Jordan (Mark

1. 9–11) Jesus knew he had a unique vocation. Then he had in a momentary vision seen the heavens open and heard the very voice of God proclaim him as Messiah in words from Ps. 2. 7–10, only to be followed by words from Isa. 42. 1–4, which made it plain that he was to be also the Servant of God who would conquer the world through gentleness and suffering.

Hard upon his baptism came the temptation in the wilderness. Matthew in his gospel (Matt. 4. 1–10) gives us a vivid and unforgettable picture of our Lord wrestling with the tempter. In a sense the three temptations Matthew mentions are the same. They all offer short cuts to success, easy ways to convince the people that Messiah has indeed come, and that Jesus is indeed he. We may imagine that Jesus' rejection of these was no instantaneous judgment but the result of long and agonising prayerful thought. After all the temptation in the desert lasted forty days – on any reckoning not an affair of a moment. We owe to St Luke's version of the temptation the suggestion that it was not a 'once only' but a recurring problem for Jesus. 'The devil departed biding his time'. (Luke 4.13)

There must have been many points in Jesus' public ministry when he was appalled by the prospect that lay ahead – one which he had himself accepted as God's will for him. It is one of these occasions, and a vital one, which we are concerned with here. For Peter, with his well-meant protest against Jesus' interpretation of his Messiahship, was simply echoing the voice of the tempter – 'Take a short cut to success'. So Jesus uses the same words to his chief supporter as he had used to the temper in the wilderness, 'Away with you, Satan', adding significantly, 'You think as men think, not as God thinks' (Matt. 16.23).

For this was the real reason for Jesus' abrupt dismissal of Peter's protest. However much he may as a robust and healthy man in the prime of life have dreaded the prospect of a cruel and horrible death at the hands of his Roman executioners, Jesus, in accepting the role of the Suffering Servant of God, had committed himself to the dread path of torture and death described by Isaiah in the fifty third chapter of his book of prophecies. Now Peter was attempting to shake his resolution and make him falter in what he saw as his divinely appointed destiny.

7

Do not throw your pearls to the pigs.

MATTHEW 7.6

Casting pearls before swine

Jesus could be quite trenchant, even violent, in his condemnation of activities of which he disapproved. 'Do not give dogs what is holy: Do not throw your pearls to the pigs.' But what did he mean? Who are the dogs and who are the pigs? Narrow-minded orthodox Jews in Jesus' day would have had no hesitation in identifying the dogs and pigs with any kind of sinners and that would include anyone who was not a Jew. These were beyond the pale, outside the covenant people, condemned to perish unless they embraced the Jewish faith and accepted the Law of Moses.

This does not seem to have been the way Jesus looked at things at all. He was not concerned with where a person was born, who his father was, or any of the other man-made compartments of race, class, colour into which we choose to divide ourselves.

There is an illuminating incident recorded in St Mark's gospel which has puzzled many people. But it helps us to understand our Lord's attitude to this whole question. It happened when Jesus was on a journey abroad. He was approached by a distraught Syrian mother who had heard of his powers and who besought him to cure her daughter. The girl had apparently some kind of mental trouble, but in accordance with well-recognised practice no Jewish healer could be expected to use his skill to restore a Gentile to sanity. In Jewish eyes the girl was an outcast and entitled to be treated as such. Jesus' first answer to the mother's request to cure her daughter sounds harsh in the extreme. His healing power was for the benefit of God's children, the Jews, and not to be thrown away on Gentile dogs. 'Let the children be satisfied first; it is not fair to take the children's bread and throw it to the dogs.' (Mark 7.27)

But the mother's love for her sick child and her quick-wittedness enabled her to see in Jesus' words not a picture of snarling curs fighting over a crust but a much more homely scene of friendly household pets being fed under the table with scraps that the children had secretly slipped down to them. Jesus had used a word which means 'puppies' and no doubt had accompanied it with a smile and a tone of voice which filled the mother's heart with hope. This unusual Jewish healer clearly did not share the normal attitude of his orthodox countrymen towards all Gentiles. So the shrewd mother used her wits to give a reply which won the Master's approval and gave her a normal healthy little girl as a reward. 'Even the puppies under the table', she said, 'eat the children's scraps.' (Mark 7. 24–30)

When Jesus spoke of casting pearls before swine he was not speaking of man-made distinctions like those of race and class but was facing realistically, as always, the fact that his followers would often come up against opposition so violent that sweet reason would be of no avail. It would be like trying to fend off snarling dogs or snapping half-wild swine. Many a missionary to this day has been met with knives and guns when his only desire was to proclaim the gospel and teach the faith.

Jesus had no illusions about the diabolical side of human nature or the devilries of which men and women are capable. Sometimes he has been misrepresented as advocating a kind of universal benevolence in a world peopled by nice friendly souls who have nothing in their thoughts but good will towards their neighbours. On the contrary, Jesus makes it plain that he sees men and women as falling into one or other of two categories. There are on the one hand those who are committed to his way of life and accept him as their Lord and Saviour. He includes with these those like the anguished father of the epileptic boy who had no illusions about the limitations of his trust in God. 'I have faith', he cried – some kind of halting, hesitant faith – 'help me where faith falls short.' (Mark 9.24) How many of us have shared the man's sense of his own inadequacy as his faltering steps failed him while he struggled to keep his feet on the pathway that leads to life! Yet our Lord tells us that all these – the fully grown in faith and those who are still learners – have God's approval and will receive his reward.

On the other hand there are those whose actions and motives are evil; and Jesus gives a comprehensive list of the black features of human behaviour – including theft, murder, adultery, greed, fraud, envy, slander and arrogance. (Mark 7. 21–22) These are the guilty ones – and it has nothing to do with race, colour, creed or social status. Jesus makes this crystal clear in his dramatic word-picture of the Last Judgement when he divides mankind into two – the sheep and the goats. (Matt. 25. 31–46) Who then are the 'sheep' who will receive the blessing of God?

They are those who fed the hungry, who befriended the stranger, who ministered to the sick, and aided the prisoner. In our more complex modern world many of these things can only be done by proxy but the motive is what matters. So let us turn to the other side of the coin. Who are the 'goats' who come under our Lord's condemnation? Jesus' categories are so simple that a child can understand them. They have nothing to do with our acceptance of creeds or indeed with our spoken beliefs at all but with our actions which speak louder than words. Did you feed the hungry, shelter the homeless, clothe the destitute, rescue the desperate? asks Jesus.

No, Lord, we mumble our excuses, but if we had only realised it was you.... Comes the crushing answer: 'Anything you did not do for one of these, however humble, you did not do for me'.

8

Your Father knows what your needs are before you ask him.
MATTHEW 6.8

Why pray?

At times Jesus seems to contradict himself. His teaching on prayer is a case in point. Here for example he seems to be discouraging us from burdening God with the trivial affairs of daily life and from asking him to help us to get what we want. He has just criticised the heathen practice of repeating the name of God over and over again as if this would ensure that their prayers would be heard. Now he says that God knows our needs and will supply them without our asking him.

Yet the same Jesus says, 'Ask, and you will receive' (Matt. 7.7); and in his parable of the importunate widow (Luke 18. 1–7) he commends the woman who keeps on pleading her case before a judge until his patience is well nigh exhausted. This story was intended to teach us to persevere in praying and never to lose heart. Moreover, in the Lord's Prayer itself, Jesus commands us to ask God to give us our daily bread (Matt. 6.11) implying that this is something we should pray for regularly day by day.

There is no doubt therefore that Jesus is encouraging us to bring our most ordinary and matter-of-fact requests and desires to God in prayer. But at the same time he is saying that God knows what our real needs are before we ask, and the two things may not coincide. Even Jesus himself, when he prayed in the Garden of Gethsemane that he might be spared the horror of

31

Calvary, had to accept that God's answer was NO; but in his humility he recognised that his Father knew best and bowed to his will.

It would seem then that Jesus leads us to a deeper understanding of prayer. He accepts that his followers, being only human and fallible men and women, will want naturally to ask their heavenly Father for the things that lie closest to their hearts and he encourages us to do so. But not only have we to recognise that some of the things we ask for are not good for us or meant for us. Jesus is teaching us here in the Sermon on the Mount that, since God knows our real needs before we lay them before him, we should ask ourselves whether our prayers are not too much concerned with requests for personal favours.

Jean Nicolas Grou in the eighteenth century had some wise words to say on this matter: 'Speaking generally, it is true to say that the necessities and accidents of life form the main subject and the actuating motive of the prayers of the ordinary Christian.' And again; 'One thing is certain: as long as you only pray to God for yourselves, your prayers will not be as perfect as he wishes them to be'. Two writers of our own day take us closer to what Jesus was saying to us. John Macquarrie makes a plea for the widest possible understanding of what prayer is about: 'Prayer is a fundamental style of thinking, passionate and compassionate, responsible and thankful, that is deeply rooted in our humanity and that manifests itself not only among believers but also among serious minded people who do not profess any religious faith'. (*Paths in Spirituality*) Bishop John Robinson in *Honest to God*, better remembered for what many saw as its undermining of the Christian faith, has this profound and helpful comment: 'The way through to the vision of the Son of man and the knowledge of God, which is the heart of contemplative prayer, is by unconditional love of the neighbour, of "the nearest THOU to hand".'

These writers, past and present, are leading us to a truer understanding of what Jesus meant by his words to the disciples on the mount – and therefore to us. Prayer is an essential part of the Christian life. We can only in a pale and subdued way echo Dietrich Bonhoeffer's cry from prison: 'O God early in the morning do I cry unto thee. Help me to pray and to think only of thee. I cannot pray alone. In me there is darkness. But with thee there is light.' *There* was a man faced with a sudden and ghastly death. But no one who has read his *Letters and Papers from Prison* can doubt that he was sustained and strengthened by prayer. With him there were no petty requests for trivial favours from God but a deep seated trust in his presence and in the support of the everlasting arms.

When Jesus said, 'Whatever you ask for in prayer, believe that you have received it and it will be yours' (Mark 11.24), he was certainly not thinking in terms of prayer for a bigger and better car, or television set, or indeed of material possessions of any kind. Christianity is not a religion of black magic. But it is a religion where things happen in response to prayer that look like magic – recovery from an apparently incurable illness, restoration of a broken marriage, an unexpected birth in a childless family. But in less dramatic ways our prayers are answered by the sense of being at peace with God, which is what reconciliation means, and as John Bunyan said, 'When thou prayest, rather let they heart be without words than thy words without heart'.

Let us look at Jesus' words again: 'Your Father knows what your needs are before you ask him' – not your 'desires' or your 'whims' or your 'fancies' but your 'needs'. God knows what we need better than we do ourselves and we may be sure that this will be granted to us. It may include some things that we do not like and may miss out some things that we feel we cannot possibly exist without; but, as Archbishop William Temple reminds us, 'God is perfect love and perfect wisdom.

We do not pray in order to change his Will, but to bring our wills into harmony with his.'

9

Be silent and come out of him.

MARK 1.25

Unclean spirits

The men and women of Jesus' day lived in a world where angels and demons formed a major part of their lives. Angels were messengers of God who did his bidding, bringing hope and comfort to those in need, protecting those who sought God's help, recording men's good deeds in God's book of life. Opposed to them were the demons or unclean spirits who were controlled by Satan, prince of darkness, and who obeyed his commands to bring evil upon mankind, especially illness. The devil and *his* angels (the Greek word simply means 'messengers') were destined for judgment and punishment at the last day. (Matt. 25.41)

All of this sounds infinitely far removed from the twentieth century. We know that among primitive people the fear of evil spirits is still very real and that witch doctors can even today strike terror into the hearts of credulous tribesmen and virtually sentence them to death by invoking the curse of demons upon them. Christian missionaries know to their cost how powerful is the pull of pagan tradition, the fear of offending tribal ancestors, and the necessity in the minds of simple people to placate the evil spirits who might at any time bring catastrophe upon their fields, their homes, and any member of their families.

But in the modern world – particularly the world of

modern medicine – have these ancient beliefs, even if
we find them in the New Testament, any more significance than other superstitions of the past such as belief
in dragons, rain-making, or casting spells? Clearly the
gospel writers believed in demon-possession and that,
when Jesus healed a madman or an epileptic, he did so
by casting out the demon who had been responsible for
the sufferer's plight.

We may take as an example the incident described at
the beginning of Mark's account of Jesus' ministry in
Galilee. (Mark 1. 21–28) Jesus had been teaching on a
Sabbath day in a synagogue at Capernaum. There was a
man in the congregation who was obviously out of his
mind or, as Mark puts it, 'possessed by an unclean
spirit'. With the intuition of a man in the grip of
demonic powers he sensed that Jesus was the Messiah.
According to Mark the demon-possessed were the first
to recognise in Jesus a more commanding authority
than that of their master Satan. Jesus cured the man of
his madness. After a violent onset of his frenzy, he was
restored to his right mind.

Our interest, however, focuses particularly on the
words spoken by Jesus which brought about the man's
recovery. As if the man had a double identity – his own
and that of the demon who had taken possession of his
body – Jesus by-passed the sufferer and addressed the
demon. 'Be silent,' he said, 'and come out of him.' It
was these words, spoken with what in Mark's view was
divine authority, which freed the man from the power of
the demon and restored him to sanity.

If we turn to the story of the stilling of the storm by
Jesus on the Lake of Galilee (Mark 4. 35–41) we may
note that Matthew and Luke in their versions of the incident say simply that Jesus rebuked the storm and the
sea became calm. (Matt. 8. 23–27 and Luke 8. 22–25)
But Mark reports that Jesus said to the sea, 'Hush, be
still,' using the same word for 'be still' as he had used in
addressing the unclean spirit in 1.25. Now we know that

the Jews, unlike the Phoenicians, were no sea-farers and thought of the sea more as a place of storms and shipwrecks (e.g. Ps. 107. 23–32) than as a highway for trade or pleasure. Doubtless Mark shared this attitude and thought of storms in the same way as he did the afflictions of disease, as caused by the malign influence of demons. But did Jesus share this view as his words here seem to suggest?

We might of course say that Mark is putting his own thoughts into the mouth of Jesus, or that if Jesus actually used these words he was accommodating himself to the language of his times and speaking in terms that were familiar to men and women of his day while not necessarily sharing their beliefs himself. But this is to evade the reality of the Incarnation. When the Word became flesh and God became man he became a true man, sharing the limited horizons of a first century Jew. It would be as unreasonable to expect Jesus to think and speak in terms of twentieth century psychiatric medicine as to expect him to be aware of the possibilities of voyages into outer space and landings on the moon. That would not be a true Incarnation.

The knowledge that Jesus had was knowledge of God and of human nature which was so far beyond that of ordinary mortals as to make him unique. This is one reason why we call him Lord and Saviour. In his knowledge of scientific facts including medical techniques, however, he thought and spoke as no more than a highly intelligent Jewish rabbi. Recognition of this fact need not disturb us or detract from our estimate of the person and work of Christ. The evidence of the gospels is beyond dispute that Jesus had a two-fold ministry, to teach and to heal the sick. It was the combined effect of his new presentation of Old Testament teaching and his compassionate response to the human suffering that surrounded him that drew the crowds of followers of whom the gospels speak.

These words from Matthew are echoed by the other

evangelists: 'He went about ... healing every disease and every infirmity among the people ... and they brought him all the sick, those afflicted with various diseases and pains, possessed by devils, epileptics, and paralytics, and he cured them.' (Matt. 4. 23–24 RSV) After the graphic description of the vast toll of human suffering and misery in this corner of the Levant come the simple words of the gospel: 'and he cured them'. Compared with this striking testimony to the healing power of Christ, does it really matter whether Jesus and his followers and patients thought in terms of 'unclean spirits'? What matters is surely that 'he cured them'.

10

May no one ever again eat fruit from you!

MARK 11.14

Jesus curses a fig-tree

St Augustine said this about the miracles of Jesus: 'Let us ask of the miracles themselves what they will tell us about Christ; for if they be but understood they have a tongue of their own. . . . He was the Word of God; and all the acts of the Word are themselves words for us; they are not as pictures, merely to look at and admire, but as letters which we must seek to read and understand.'

Alan Richardson in *The Miracle-Stories of the Gospels* adds this: 'There can be little doubt that the makers of the Gospel tradition understood the miracles of Jesus as "signs" or symbolical acts which convey in a dramatised form essential Christological teaching.'

But what kind of teaching is conveyed by this story of the 'cursing of the fig tree' – a story so reminiscent of the kind of thing we read of in the apocryphal gospels as to make us wonder whether this is not an early specimen of the fantasies of the writers of these second and third century attempts to give glory to God and his Son, by repeating hearsay gossip of what marvellous things had been done in Palestine by the Saviour when he was on earth?

Yet the cold facts have to be faced. This story in Mark's gospel is as firmly embedded in gospel tradition as his account of the events of Holy Week. But what are

39

we to make of it? May we look at it again?

In Holy Week on the day after Jesus' entry into Jerusalem when he had spent the night with his friends at Bethany, a couple of miles away, he walked into the Holy City. On the way in, he felt hungry and noticing in the distance a fig-tree in leaf, he went to see if he could find anything on it. But when he came there he found nothing but leaves; for it was not the season for figs. It was then that he uttered the words which are at the head of this chapter. What are we to make of them?

This is one of the most puzzling – if not *the* most puzzling of the sayings of Jesus. Why should he put a curse on the unoffending fig-tree which according to Mark had completely withered by the next morning? (Mark 11.20) If the whole story is a legend, there is no problem. But is it a legend? Historically the incident is convincingly fixed in the narrative of Holy Week. But we are told by knowledgable travellers, to say nothing of Mark himself, that Eastertide is the wrong time of year to look for figs. How then can we account for Jesus' apparently petulant outburst?

It has been suggested that the origin of the story is to be found in the existence of an isolated withered fig-tree which stood by the roadside between Bethany and Jerusalem in gospel times, round which the story had grown that its condition had been brought about by having a curse placed upon it by Jesus as Mark records. This explanation surely smacks of nineteenth century rationalism. A more likely line of thought is to connect the story with St Luke's parable in ch. 13.6–9. As Luke tells us there, Jesus spoke of the owner of a vineyard who had a fig-tree growing among his vines and who after a series of disappointing years when the tree had borne no fruit ordered his vine-dresser to cut it down. In response to his employee's plea he agreed to give the tree a last chance to produce a good crop of fruit the following year.

Since Israel was often referred to in the Old Testament under the symbol of a fig-tree or a vineyard it is clear that Jesus in his parable was attacking the orthodox Jewish religion of his day as a barren tree that bore no fruit and but for the mercy of God deserved to be destroyed. Empty ceremonies, arid disputations, theological hair-splitting, in answering the problems of ordinary folk in Palestine about real life – this was what tried the patience of Jesus and called forth his condemnation.

So we come back to the incident of the withered fig-tree – which now appears as an acted parable but also as a stage nearer to the dénouement. Jesus is in Jerusalem. He has thrown down the gauntlet, challenging the Jewish religious experts on their own ground. Messiah has come to his inheritance – foretold by prophet after prophet. But whereas during his Galilean ministry he spoke, in his parable of the fig-tree in Luke 13. 6–9, of the possibility of Israel's reform, he had with the imminence of the Crucifixion conceded that for old Israel's religion there was no hope. It was finished. Messiah had come, but the Jewish hierarchy had turned its back and was even now plotting his death.

Yet condemnation was never our Lord's last word. Forgiveness for his enemies was in his heart and on his lips even in the agony of the Cross. (Luke 23.34) Israel was God's chosen people, chosen to be an example to the rest of the world and to lead the Gentiles into the way of truth. Time and again they had failed, and had chosen to disregard and defy the counsel and warnings of the prophets who had called for national repentance. Some prophets, like Amos, had declared that God's patience was exhausted and that nothing but retribution lay ahead. In the name of God Amos had declared, 'I have my eyes on this sinful kingdom and I will wipe it off the face of the earth.' (Amos 9.8) Yet even Amos in the end had been unable to believe that Israel had no future and had foreseen a time of restoration and renewal. (Amos 9. 11–15).

But Jesus who shared the compassion of Jeremiah for

his people and the hopes of Isaiah for a more glorious future believed that with his own ministry the age to come had already dawned. The mountain of Jewish unbelief would yet be removed (Mark 11. 23), and the barren fig-tree would yet bear fruit. (Luke 13. 8–9)

11

You are not far from the Kingdom of God.

MARK 12.34

Getting our priorities right

Jesus in Jerusalem during Holy Week was involved in disputation mostly with his enemies who sought to trap him in argument. (Mark 12. 13–27) He successfully routed their attacks but the last challenge was of a different kind and came not from a hostile questioner but from a man whom we would now call a sympathetic enquirer. This man was a lawyer, which in New Testament terms does not mean an expert in making wills, settling estates, transferring property or preparing cases for the law courts. A lawyer was an expert in interpreting the Law of Moses and all its ramifications and developments. This could be a much more sterile occupation than trying to settle any legal disputes today.

The particular lawyer in the gospel narrative of Holy Week had been an attentive listener to the Pharisees' and Sadducees' loaded questions to Jesus, and to our Lord's impressive handling of them. He now asked him a question of a different sort. The man was obviously not seeking to score points or to outwit Jesus as the other questioners had been, but to get an answer to a problem which had been troubling him. Moses had originally given the people ten commandments as God's guide to the good life. These had been analysed, dissected, amended, qualified and expanded by the Jewish religious authorities over the years until by the time of

Jesus there were said to be 613 commandments which laid down the rules for conduct, either to be practised or shunned, which any devout Jew must observe. All of them were held to be divinely ordained.

This made life extremely confusing for ordinary people who tended to leave these difficult matters to the Pharisees. But even St Paul, who before his conversion was a law-abiding Pharisee, confessed that the power of sin within himself defeated his best efforts. (Rom. 7. 19–20) Perhaps this lawyer in the gospel story had shared Paul's disillusionment. At all events here he asks Jesus which of all the many commandments was the most important. 'Which commandment is first of all?' he asks (Mark 12.28)

Jesus, without hesitation, quoted the words of Deut. 6. 4 which formed part of the Jewish Creed, recited morning and evening by all faithful Jews, preserved as a constant reminder on their wrists and foreheads, on their doorposts and on their gates: 'The Lord our God is the only Lord: love the Lord your God with all your heart, with all your soul, with all your mind, and with all your strength.'

Throughout the centuries from the time of Moses, amid the multiplicity of gods and goddesses, the allurements of the fertility cults of Canaan, the magnificence of the temples of Assyria, Babylon, Persia and now the all-pervasive might of the cults of Greece and Rome, this tiny indomitable handful of Jews had maintained their faith in the uniqueness of their God – lived for it, died for it, suffered untold hardship and victimisation for it. Now Jesus sets his seal upon it as the primary commandment of the Old Testament Law, which he hands on to his followers to honour. Total commitment to God is then, according to Jesus, the greatest commandment of all. He quickly adds a second which he brackets with the first. It is also a quotation from the Old Testament from the book of Leviticus 19.18: 'You shall love your neighbour as a man like yourself'. It is

buried in the same chapter among a miscellany of regulations for the proper offering of animal sacrifice, permitted sexual relationships, kosher meat, wizards, hair
cutting, correct weights and measures. All were equally
binding, equally demanding obedience. It has been said
that in singling out the commandments concerning our
duty to God and our neighbour from the total of 613 and
making them into a joint and unique obligation, Jesus
set aside the other 612.

The lawyer in the gospel story eagerly accepted and
welcomed Jesus' answer to his question (Mark 12. 32–
33) and added 'that is far more than any burnt offerings
or sacrifices'. It is clear from his words that his real
problem, and what had prompted his question, was his
impatience with the emphasis of the rigorists among the
Jewish rabbis upon the necessity of swallowing the Law
as a whole – moral precepts *and* ceremonial regulations.
There were many who shared the more liberal views of
Rabbi Hillel, roughly contemporary with Jesus, who
said: 'Do not to another what thou wouldest not that he
should do to thee; this is the whole law, the rest is commentary'. If this splendid revolutionary thinker had
been heeded, much blood need not have been shed and
much bitterness might have been avoided.

As things worked out, Judaism and Christianity,
which had so much in common took different roads and
established a pattern which exists to the present day.
Orthodox Judaism tended to become more arid, while
liberal Judaism lost the backbone which the Law had
provided and became a flabby accommodation to the
ways of the world. This has been the case in the West.
Only in modern Israel itself, glorying in its new-found
freedom, can be seen something of the old fire and
passion which the prophets had kindled. Religious
orthodoxy has tended to become a veneer, and self-
assertive nationalism has become the new faith for the
twentieth century Zealots.

Yet Hillel and his disciples, such as the lawyer in our

story, have left their mark on Jewish thought and Christian practice. However imperfectly we succeed in fulfilling the two great commandments which unite Christians and Jews in a common service and remind us of our joint debt to the Old Testament, we have, especially in recent years, become more and more conscious of what unites us than of what divides us. We may perhaps take the words of Jesus to the lawyer which stand at the head of this chapter as the key to greater Jewish-Christian understanding. They were spoken to a Jew but they are words which any Christian would be proud to think that our Lord could say also to him: 'You are not far from the kingdom of God'.

12

The part that Mary has chosen is best.

LUKE 10.42

Martha and Mary

The scene is a house in Bethany, just outside Jerusalem, which gospel evidence and tradition identify as the home of Lazarus and his two sisters Martha and Mary. Jesus came there in the course of his ministry, as he was to do in the critical days of Passion Week when he lodged with this family. We are told that Martha, who appears to have been the manager of the household, being probably the eldest of the family, welcomed Jesus to her home. While she busied herself with domestic chores, including the preparation of a meal, Mary, the younger sister, had seated herself at Jesus' feet and was listening to his words with rapt attention.

Martha resented the fact that she was left to do all the work while her sister, she felt, was idling away her time listening to their distinguished visitor. She complained to Jesus who, however, defended Mary, claiming that her apparent inactivity was in reality more truly service of the Lord than Martha's busyness about the house.

The story, including Jesus' words at the head of this chapter, has been much misunderstood. By some it has been taken to be extolling the value of a life of prayer and contemplation over a life of active sharing in the work of the world, whether in the home or in factory or office. Martha has been praised as the practical worka-day woman, compared with Mary the dreamy intellectual or bluestocking. This is to miss the point of the story. Martha was not an efficient practical housewife. Jesus would have had nothing but praise for that. No, she was a fusspot – and a querulous one to boot!

Jesus had come in from the heat and dust of country roads, footsore and weary and exhausted from the exacting life of preaching and healing which he had taken upon himself. He needed and wanted rest, and peace and understanding. And here was Martha, with the best will in the world, clattering around, organising an elaborate meal for the important visitor, when all he wanted was to relax and talk quietly among friends. Mary was sensitive enough to know this. Her great gift was to be a good listener.

When Jesus said in reply to Martha's complaints 'but one thing is necessary' he proably meant that he wanted no more than a simple meal and not Martha's elaborate spread. We must avoid the temptation to turn the day-to-day incidents of our Lord's Galilean ministry into sweeping generalisations valid for all times and for all situations. When Jesus said to the rich young ruler (Matt. 19. 16–22) 'sell all that you have and give to the poor' this was not a dictum applicable to all, but a particular instruction addressed to a specific enquirer with a personal problem – his obsession with money.

Similarly it would be quite wrong to magnify this homely incident of Martha and Mary into a wide-ranging discussion about the advantages and disadvantages of the contemplative and practical ways of life. Both are essential parts of the witness and work of the Church. Mary was commended for her tact, for knowing that she was privileged to listen to the Master, for giving him the quietness he needed. Martha on the other hand was rushing around 'fretting and fussing' and no doubt providing a running commentary on what was going on around her.

There is a Hindu saying which runs like this: 'He who sees how action may be rest and rest action; he is wisest among his kind; he has the truth. He does well – acting or resting.' The motto of the Benedictines says the same thing in a different way: 'to work is to pray'. For there are these two sides to the Christian life and they are complementary. Christian writers have tended to concentrate on prayer rather than work. Our Victorian grandfathers who believed strongly in the gospel of hard work tended at the same time to rate it decidedly lower than personal and public piety. Church and chapel going, prayer meetings, and family worship formed the pattern of life in which the old age pensioners of today were brought up.

Let me quote from two masters of the English and Scottish traditions: Bishop Russell Barry in his *Christian Ethics and Secular Society* says: 'Contemplation is not in itself "more spiritual" than recording a vote or managing a business'. While Dr A. C. Craig, Moderator of the General Assembly of the Church of Scotland, maintains in his *University Sermons:* 'There is a kind of of Church worker for whom our age even more urgently calls, and on whom the life and example of Christ set more immediately the seal of discipleship – the man who, to the glory of God and for the good of his fellows, does honest work of the everyday sort'.

Archbishop William Temple tells of an occasion in a railway carriage where his companions were a well-meaning evangelist and a man recognisable as a baker from the flour on his clothes. The evangelist, anxious to save another soul, asked the man, who confessed to being a Christian, what he did for Christ – hoping to be told that he took part in gospel meetings, taught in a Sunday School, or helped with youth work of some kind. But the man stolidly insisted that his service of Christ was to bake the best bread he could. The Archbishop gave this answer his unqualified approval. And so, we may guess, would our Lord himself have done.

Jesus' preference for the 'way of Mary' was no reflection on the 'Way of Martha' if we mean by that, as most people do, the efforts of housewives to make their homes places of fulfilment and renewal for their families – young and old alike. The truth is surely that every Martha needs on occasion to play the part of Mary and to know when to do it.

13

Go and do as he did.

LUKE 10.37

The good Samaritan

Probably of all the parables that Jesus told in the course of his ministry the two best known are those of the 'good Samaritan' and the prodigal son. Both are to be found only in the third gospel. Among the many homely illustrations that Jesus gave of his message of the Good News these two crystallise his teaching most completely. Yet for many readers of the gospels today they are not without their own difficulties.

St Luke tells us that the parable of the good Samaritan was the result of a question to our Lord by an anonymous lawyer. (Luke 10.25) If we read there the words of this earnest enquirer, we inevitably ask ourselves: Was this the same lawyer who according to Mark (12. 28 ff.) asked Jesus which of the commandments was the most important? In this case the lawyer's question is, 'Master, what must I do to inherit eternal life?' and he answers his own question by quoting Jesus' words in reply to the query about which commandment was greatest of all. Whether the questioners on these two occasions were identical or not, the questions themselves were put to Jesus in a friendly way which was far removed from the normally hostile approaches of the religious authorities, which were more designed to entrap Jesus than to elicit his opinion.

This lawyer (whom we would nowadays call a theologian – see ch. 11) who had got the answer to his question as to how to inherit eternal life had still another problem. Jesus had said, 'Love your neighbour as yourself,' but that raised yet another question, 'Who is my neighbour?' This was a real difficulty for liberal-minded Jews. Orthodoxy required them to exclude from the concept of 'neighbour' almost everybody except rigid upholders of the Law and that meant a ban on association with Gentiles above all, but also with Samaritans, who had been for centuries at enmity with Jerusalem and all that its temple stood for.

In his parable of the Good Samaritan, which was Jesus' reply to the lawyer's question, our Lord cut across all these legalistic and traditional distinctions and came down on the side of basic human need. The story is so well known that it hardly requires re-telling. The traveller on the dangerous road from Jerusalem to Jericho – attacked by robbers – beaten up and left for dead by the roadside – three others are making the same journey – two are professional ecclesiastics who 'pass by on the other side' for fear of ritual contamination from a corpse – the third, a despised Samaritan, stops and tends the victim's injuries – takes him to an inn – pays for his keep – promises the landlord to make good any deficit on his return journey.

Having told this simple story Jesus asks the lawyer which of the three travellers behaved like a true neighbour to the wounded man. The lawyer's reply was 'the one who showed him kindness'. To this Jesus retorted briefly: 'Go and do as he did'. This may have solved the lawyer's problem but it raises difficulties for us today. It has been pointed out that the good Samaritan had everything on his side. He had a spare mule; there was an inn at hand; he had enough money to pay for the injured man's lodging as well as his own; he could guarantee to settle any outstanding debt since he would soon be back again. Not everyone who tries to comply with our Lord's instruction by emulating the example of the good Samaritan is as well equipped with the where-withal as he was.

But surely Jesus did not intend his command to be taken literally? The early Christian Fathers in their efforts to find mystical significance in this as in other homely illustrations that Jesus used in his teaching, identified the innkeeper with the Church, the two silver pieces which the Samaritan gave him for the wounded man's keep meant the two chief sacraments, and the Samaritan's promise to return stood for the Second Coming. Less fanciful and more akin to the mind and purpose of Jesus was St Jerome's identification of Jesus with the good Samaritan, and of himself and other souls in need of help and comfort as the traveller who 'fell among thieves'.

This was his prayer: 'Show thy mercy to me, O Lord, to glad my heart withal. Lo, here the man that was caught of thieves, wounded, and left for half-dead, as he was going towards Jericho. Thou kind-hearted Samaritan, take me up.'

But none of this solves our problem, which is how far can we follow in our Lord's footsteps and obey his commands in the twentieth century world which is so radically different from the world in which Jesus lived. We have seen that in the case of the good Samaritan we cannot recreate the exact situation in which he found himself. We cannot therefore take Jesus' words to the lawyer, 'Go and do as he did,' to be literally binding on ourselves. But we can fulfil the spirit of our Lord's injunction even if we cannot fulfil it to the letter.

St Teresa of Avila said: 'We cannot know whether we love God, although there may be strong reasons for thinking so, but there can be no doubt about whether we love our neighbour or no.' The Samaritan was not, and could not because of his background, be regarded as the 'neighbour' of the wounded man but he behaved towards him in a neighbourly way. That was what mattered. The lawyer in Jesus' parable had himself given the only possible answer to his own question, Who is my neighbour? Of the three men on the Jericho road only one was a true neighbour to the casualty lying by the wayside. He was as the lawyer had said 'the one who showed him kindness'. This is what Jesus really meant when he said, 'Go and do as he did'. Our neighbour is just anyone who needs our help.

In the words of Sydney Carter's fine hymn:

When I needed a neighbour, were you there, were you there?
And the creed and the colour and the name won't matter, Were you there?

14

Your brother . . . was lost and is found.

LUKE 15.32

The prodigal son

One of the most popular musical 'hits' recently has, surprisingly, both because of its name 'Amazing Grace' and its theme, which is the same as that of the parable of the prodigal son, become a record-breaker with teenagers as well as with middle aged church-folk. While it would be too much to claim that this heralds a religious revival, it does suggest that the message of the parable gets home to the young generation of the twentieth century because so many of them can identify with the ne'er-do-well son.

Like Jesus' story of the good Samaritan his tale of the prodigal son is so well known as to have become proverbial. The younger brother, impatient with an unadventurous life on the farm, sets off with his share of the family fortune to see the world. He comes to grief, partly through his own extravagance and partly through an economic disaster. Starvation drives him to swallow his pride and throw himself on his father's mercy. To his astonishment he is welcomed home by his father with open arms and the 'fatted calf' is killed in celebration. The old man treats him like one who has come back from the dead. He was lost but now he is found.

The elder brother (like Martha in real life (see chapter 12)) takes strong exception to what he regards as unfair favouritism towards a younger member of the family, refers angrily to the prodigal as 'this son of yours' who has wasted his father's money on women, and is now regaled with the 'fatted calf.' He on the other hand claims that he has 'slaved' on the farm all his life with little thanks.

Although Jesus was no doubt thinking of the Pharisees when he caricatured them as the elder brother, the parallel between the elder brother and Martha is worth attention since it is part of the problem of this story for twentieth century readers of the gospels. Both of them are representative of the good, hardworking, solid, faithful members of their family and of the community, whose unspectacular service keeps society on an even keel. Most of the readers of this book are not likely to be classed with the prodigal son. They are more akin to the elder brother.

They have done a good job of work in whatever field they have chosen or where their lot has chanced to place them. Understandably they feel, even if they do not say so openly, that having tried to be good fathers or mothers to their children, loyal sons or daughters to ageing parents, they deserve something better than to be given second place when some other member of the family returns home after what was perhaps a more exciting and colourful life in distant parts of the world where he had gone to seek his fortune. But as the father in the story says to the elder brother, 'My boy, you are always with me, and everything I have is yours'. Life has its own compensations for the faithful stay-at-homes.

Did Jesus mean us to think of the elderly father as representing God? It is perhaps more likely that he intended this old man's welcome to his wayward son to suggest God's love for all sorts and conditions of men including penitent sinners. All of us who are relatively law-abiding, church-going citizens are bound to share something of the elder brother's resentment. His younger brother has had it both ways. He 'lived it up' as

long as the money lasted, while the elder brother kept
the farm going, and then the prodigal came home to a
royal welcome. Surely this was unfair!

But the elder brother had overlooked the misery that
the prodigal had endured when his money ran out.
Faced with starvation he was glad to find a job as a
swineherd – particularly abhorrent to a Jew – and was
thankful for a share of the pigs' food. He had paid the
price of his folly, but his physical plight was more than
matched by his unendurable remorse in which self-pity
played no small part. 'Living it up' had cost him dearly
indeed!

At last, as we are told, he 'came to his senses' and
decided to admit that he had been a fool. The most he
hoped for was to be given a menial job on the family
farm. He knew he deserved no better. His repentance
was genuine and complete. He says to his father, 'I have
sinned against God and against you; I am no longer fit to
be called your son.' When he got near his old home his
father had seen him a long way off: had run out to meet
him: embraced him: exchanged his tattered rags for
decent clothing and gave orders for the welcoming feast
to begin.

In contrast to the elder brother's description of the
prodigal as 'this son of yours' the father speaks of him as
'your brother' and receives him back into the family as
one who had been dead and had come back to life, who
had been lost and had now been found. Whether this
would have been our own reaction in similar circum-
stances, the message of the Gospel is that this is what it
ought to be.

George MacLeod tells a moving story of a twentieth
century Prodigal – a misfit who had been in and out of
prison and had more or less reconciled himself to spend-
ing the rest of his life 'inside'. Convicted of almost every
crime in the calendar except murder he was visited in
prison by his mother who said, 'John, it doesn't matter
what you have done or what you do I'm still your

mother and I'll stand by you.' Afterwards he said, 'Well, if my mother's like that, I can believe what they tell me about God.'

15

How many loaves have you?

Feeding the multitude

The feeding of the five thousand and of the four thousand recorded in St Mark's Gospel has raised questions in many minds. These miracles are reported in Mark 6. 30–44 and 8. 1–9. Suggestions that Mark has made two separate miracles out of one do not help us very much, and he is unlikely to have forgotten by chapter 8 that he had already told of a similar incident in chapter 6. For some readers of the gospels these stories present no problem. Jesus, as the Son of God, they would say, was perfectly capable of multiplying the five loaves and two fish so that there was enough and to spare to satisfy the hunger of this vast crowd.

Others will remember that from the time of the temptation in the wilderness after his baptism, Jesus had set his face against winning support for his cause, and popularity for himself, by turning stones into loaves, or throwing himself down from the parapet of the temple (Matt. 4. 1–7) and thereafter had steadfastly refused to accede to all requests that he should prove his Messiahship by giving some dramatic 'sign' from heaven. (Luke 11. 29)

It has been suggested by some modern writers that what happened was that Jesus and his disciples set an example to the crowd by sharing what provisions they had brought with them, whereupon the crowd were shamed into dividing their own packed lunches among those who had come unprepared, so that in the end as the gospel says 'they all ate and were satisfied'. Others again have pointed out that no miracle was called for since, as the disciples themselves had suggested, the crowd could have foraged for themselves in the houses and villages nearby and bought what they needed.

But St Mark's account of the feeding of the five thousand and of the four thousand irresistibly suggests comparison with his narrative of the Last Supper in chapter 14 verses 22 ff. Jesus takes the bread in his hands, asks a blessing, breaks the bread and distributes it to the people. Are we not then dealing with sacramental occasions rather than with the miraculous multiplication of five loaves and two fishes? Fish was the staple diet of those who lived near the Lake of Galilee and primitive Christian art indicates that bread and fish featured together in early celebrations of the Eucharist.

But why does St Mark record two separate feedings? Here we may note the significance of the different numbers involved. On the first occasion (chapter 6), five thousand partook and twelve baskets of fragments were left over. 'Five' was a distinctively Jewish number – based on the five books of the Law – and 'twelve' was the number of the tribes of Israel. On the second occasion (ch. 8) there were seven loaves and seven baskets of fragments. 'Seven' is in the New Testament the characteristically Gentile number. There were seven deacons (Acts 6. 3), and there was the mission of the seventy. (Luke 10. 1ff) In earlier times the nations of the world were traditionally divided into seventy, and the Greek translation of the Old Testament, the Septuagint, was designed for Jews who could no longer read Hebrew and was so called because it was said to have been the work of seventy scholars. It has also been pointed out that the word used for 'basket' in Mark 6 is the Jewish word, whereas in Mark 8 it is the ordinary word for a 'basket' used by Greek-speaking Gentiles.

Mark therefore surely wanted us to see in the two stories the message that the Eucharist is for Jews and Gentiles, foreshadowed in Galilee and the Decapolis (7. 31) but fulfilled in Jerusalem for the whole company of Christian believers. We are therefore dealing with what might be called a Galilean Lord's Supper.

But there is more to it than that. Mark emphasises the fact that Jesus took the disciples to task for their failure to understand the deeper significance of his feeding of the multitudes. (8. 14–21) Mark clearly sees them as signs of the Messiah. Soon, near Caesarea Philippi, Peter was to confess Jesus as the Messiah, the Christ, an avowal which Jesus acclaimed as a direct revelation from God. (Matt. 16. 13 ff) But here Jesus is preparing the disciples' minds for that moment. The gradual recovery of sight in the healing of the blind man of Bethsaida, which Mark relates at this point, (8.22–25), is clearly intended to suggest a parallel with the opening of the disciples' eyes to the truth about who their Master really was.

The feeding of the multitude is recorded in all four gospels, underlining its peculiar significance and importance. But it is in St John's version that we find the implications most fully expressed. (John 6. 1–14) In Old Testament times Moses had made so great an impact upon the life of Israel that the expectation was that one day God would raise up a prophet like Moses to speak in his name to the people. (Deut. 18. 17) Moses had been associated in people's minds with what they saw as the miracle of manna in the wilderness, the bread from heaven. (Exod. 16) It was thus natural to connect the feeding of the multitude with the manna from heaven and to identify Jesus with the prophet like Moses who was to come into the world (John 6. 14).

We may also note that another notable Old Testament figure, Elisha, is reported to have fed a hundred men with twenty barley loaves. They were satisfied and there was some bread left over. (2 Kgs 4. 42–44) As

Alan Richardson points out in *The Miracle-Stories of the Gospels*, 'Elisha, upon whom Elijah's mantle had fallen, must be regarded as the shadow of which Elijah is the substance,' and we remember that at the Transfiguration (Mark 9. 2–8) Jesus stood talking with Moses and Elijah on the Mount of Transfiguration.

For the gospel writers, as for St Paul, the Old Testament pointed forward to Christ as the fulfilment of the Law and the Prophets. They saw too in the testing-time of the early Israelites in the desert, where they were sustained by manna, the bread from heaven, and water miraculously, as it seemed, produced from the rock which Moses struck (Num. 20), foreshadowings of the Messiah. Christ, said St Paul, had been the supernatural rock which accompanied Israel's travels (1 Cor. 10. 4) refreshing them with the water of life. Now the new Israel is being represented by the Lord's Body and Blood in the Eucharist.

PART TWO

16

Do not suppose that I have come to abolish the Law and the prophets; I did not come to abolish, but to complete.

MATTHEW 5.17

Jesus and the law

The man who blandly declares, 'My religion is the Sermon on the Mount', must have a key to understanding which is denied to the ordinary Bible-reader. For the sermon contains several difficult sayings, and this statement about the law is perhaps the most difficult. And the difficulty continues into verse 18: 'I tell you this: so long as heaven and earth endure, not a letter, not a stroke, will disappear from the Law before all that it stands for is achieved' (I here follow NEB's marginal reading, which is closer to what I consider the correct meaning).

The passage appears to undermine all our convictions about Jesus removing the Jewish law as a path to salvation. And it conflicts with his own willingness to flout the law when he healed on the sabbath, ate with people who were ceremonially unclean, and opposed the divorce laws handed down from Moses. (Mark 3.1–6; 2.15–17; 10.1–12) But perhaps this observation that Jesus often seemed to ignore or even reject the law as Jews understood it will provide for us a way into grasping why Jesus spoke like this and what he meant.

For we can imagine that Jesus' attitudes and actions could quickly create the impression that he was attempting to lower the demands of God and letting people of dubious character enter the family of God 'on the cheap'. That is the worry which respectable religious people always have when anyone tries to offer the friendship of God to society's outcasts. Jesus would certainly need to make it clear that – whilst he opposed the Pharisees' obsession with legal correctness – he was by no means diluting the demands of God or offering 'cheap grace'.

On several occasions he stressed that God's requirements are more, not less, demanding than the law as his contemporaries understood it. (See, for example, Matt. 19.16–22; 23.3–4, 23–24). Similarly, in Matt. 5.17ff. Jesus was defending himself against the charge that he was undercutting God's demands. The way that the statement is phrased indicates that a specific accusation is being related – '*Do not suppose* that I have come to abolish . . . .'

However, there is more to it than this. Since the law of Moses was the central feature of Jewish life, it was essential for Jesus to explain his relationship to it. That is what these verses, and the series of contrasts which follow in Matt. 5, are doing. Jesus has not come to abolish the law or the prophets. Incidentally, although the law is the main theme of the passage, the prophets are mentioned because they too, like the law, include moral commands. Similarly, in Matt. 7.12 and 22.40 the command to love is said to summarise the law and the prophets.

Jesus came, he says, not to abolish but to 'fulfil' or 'complete' the law. This is the central problem of the passage: what does Jesus mean by 'fulfil'? If we can understand that, we shall understand how Jesus saw his relationship to the law – and hence to Jewish religion. The term 'fulfil' implies both discontinuity and continuity with the past. There is discontinuity, because the teaching of Jesus *goes beyond* what was there in the law. It *completes* what was previously incomplete. We see this in the contrasting declarations of Matt. 5.21–48:

'You have learned . . . But what I tell you is this . . . .'
There is a new quality, a fuller demand, in the message
of Jesus.

But there is also continuity, because the law *pointed
forward* to the message of Jesus. Elsewhere Jesus says
that both law and prophets *prophesied* until the time of
John the Baptist (Matt. 11.13). When he says that he
fulfils the law, he is speaking of fulfilment in the same
sense as when he talks of fulfilling prophecy. The prophets pointed forward to the mission and actions of
Jesus. The law pointed forward to his teaching. Jesus
fulfils the law in the sense that his teaching about the
demand of God was foreshadowed by the Old Testament law. His teaching goes beyond the law, yet the law
was pointing in the same direction.

This theme is continued in verse 18, with its insistence
that not a letter or a stroke will disappear from the law.
The letter ('jot' in the King James Version) is the small-
est letter in the Hebrew alphabet. The stroke ('tittle')
probably represents a decorative stroke attached to
some letters. Not even the tiniest detail of the law will
become invalid – until two things happen. Firstly, it will
remain valid 'so long as heaven and earth endure'. That
is probably a colourful way of saying how hard it is for
the law to pass away. Secondly, the law will remain
valid until 'all that it stands for is achieved'. We have
already seen how the law pointed forward to Jesus'
teaching. Now this sentence means that the demands of
the law are about to reach their ultimate expression in
the message of Jesus. The law is not abolished, but it
receives its full and valid expression not merely in its
own continued existence, but in the demands of the
kingdom of God as expressed in Jesus' life and message.
Hence he goes on immediately to stress that his followers' righteousness must go beyond that of the scribes
and Pharisees, and to illustrate how the demand of
God's kingdom goes beyond the requirement of the law
(Matt. 5.19–48).

What began as a statement about Jesus' relationship to the Jewish law has turned out to be a statement about the law's relation to Jesus. For Jesus is the central figure. With a commanding authority he unfolds the will of the God whose kingdom he brings near to men: 'But what I tell you is this . . .' He is in fact claiming to be bringing the final revelation of God and his will. And he is calling for obedience to his own teaching as no one had dared before. That he claims total superiority over the law is clear if we set his statement here alongside another one. Here he says, 'So long as heaven and earth endure' nothing will disappear from the law. But in Matt. 24.35 he says, 'Heaven and earth will pass away; my words will never pass away'.

17

*Do not be anxious about tomorrow; tomorrow will look
after itself:
Each day has troubles enough of its own.*

MATTHEW 6.34

Cure for worry

A first reaction to this saying might be to suggest that it
shows a pessimistic side of Jesus. It presents us with an
attitude of resignation in face of the uncertainties of life.
It advises us not to worry about tomorrow for the simple
reason that today brings us quite enough problems to
cope with. It is conventional wisdom, born out of hard
experience. Certainly Jesus' saying has parallels in the
sayings of Jewish rabbis, 'Do not be anxious for
tomorrow,' said one, 'for you do not know what a day
may bring forth. Perhaps tomorrow you will be dead,
and so will have worried about what has ceased to be
any concern of yours'. And another: 'Each hour has
enough trouble of its own'. Practical, proverbial sayings
such as this are not to be despised. Often they restore a
sense of perspective and bring us back to a commonsense approach to life just when it is most needed. Yet
we need more than commonsense if life is to have its full
meaning.

A second reaction, and a very common one, is to say
that Jesus was being quite unrealistic in urging us not to
be anxious about tomorrow. Surely it is sheer folly to
think only of today? We have been misled here by the
words of the King James Version, 'Take no thought for

the morrow'. In the seventeenth century 'take no thought' meant 'do not be anxious', whereas in the twentieth century it sounds like an exhortation to make no plans for the future. Parables such as those involving stewards and servants (for example, Matt. 24. 43–47; Luke 12. 42–44) presuppose that orderly planning for the future is a sensible part of running a household. Jesus assumes that it was right for parents to provide for the needs of their children (Matt. 7.11) and children for their parents (Mark 7. 9–13). And the rich fool who in the parable (Luke 12. 16–21) enlarged his barns to make room for a bumper harvest is condemned not because he provided for the future but because he did so without thought of God or of his own mortality.

Jesus taught in effect that there are two ways of living for the future. There is, first, the prudent planning which is itself an expression of confidence and hope in God's good purposes for the world, a refusal to panic in the face of present uncertainty or catastrophe. Jesus expressed this attitude himself when, with the shadow of the cross before him, he prepared his disciples for the time beyond his crucifixion and promised 'to go before them into Galilee'. (Mark 14. 28)

The second way of living for the future, which Jesus condemns, is the way of anxiety, the failure to trust. You see it in the person who believes that the only way to secure happiness for the future is by concentrating on the collection of money and possessions. An opinion poll conducted in the United States in the nineteen-sixties revealed that most people expected to find happiness through greater material prosperity. When a similar poll was taken ten years later did they find that increased material prosperity had produced greater happiness? Of course not, for this method of removing anxiety brings its own anxieties with it.

You see this wrong way of living for the future also in those who refuse to recognise the present for what it is and to live in it realistically. For example, there is the girl who so longs to be married that she lives in a fantasy world, and the present with all its joys and possibilities just passes her by.

Against all this Jesus said, 'Do not be anxious'. But what use is it to say that? Telling people not to worry is likely to make them worry more, not less. But this is where Jesus goes beyond conventional wisdom. For the saying which we are considering is not really command, but gospel. It arises from all that Jesus has been saying in the previous verses about the care of God for his children. It is interesting that Jewish rabbis explicitly forbade prayers that God's mercy should extend 'even to the bird's nest'. It was considered disrespectful to link God's care with a mere bird. Yet Jesus declared that God's care embraces even the sparrows which are sold two a penny. (Matt. 1. 29–31) And here in Matt. 6 he points to the birds and flowers as objects of God's concern, adding that his concern for human beings is so much greater.

Deliverance from worry is possible for whose who are willing to trust in the Father who cares about what his children need. They receive each day as a gift from him. They see him as the ultimate creator and source of all good things. They use the Lord's prayer to turn this trust into prayer: 'Give us today our daily bread' (Matt. 6.11). For they know that anxiety about the basic needs of life is one of the things that can hinder the coming of God's rule and kingdom in their lives. The only way to provide sensibly for tomorrow without succumbing to anxiety is to live by the command of Matt. 6.33: 'Set your mind on God's kingdom and his justice before everything else, and all the rest will come to you as well'.

But we dare not be sentimental about this. Jesus' talk about God's care was certainly no guarantee of protection from all harm. He promised safety through death, not necessarily from death. He knew that the birds of the air often have a hard life, and the lilies of the field get trampled on. And we know that there are people in the world for whom 'daily bread' would be an unprecedented luxury. Jesus did not gloss over this. He acknowledged the 'troubles' which each day brings forth. But his message about God's kingdom meant that the final removal of such sufferings *was* on the way, and that the knowledge of God as Father enables men to retain hope so as to seek a fulness of life for all mankind. 'While there's life there's hope', we often say. We might do better to say, 'While there's hope, there's life.'

18

Animal kingdom

From Aesop's fables to Mickey Mouse, people have always been fascinated by comparisons between humans and animals. And here in a single verse we have a whole menagerie. It is part of Jesus' instructions as he sent out the twelve on a mission of preaching and healing. It is wrong, perhaps, to classify it as a 'difficult' saying, but it is well worth studying.

The saying leads into a passage about the danger, the opposition and persecution which the raw missionaries are liable to face, and must be understood against that background. Let us take each animal in turn, beginning with the biggest. Wolves in Jesus' teaching sometimes symbolise the general menace which threatens his followers (John 10.12). Or they may be false prophets – 'men who come to you dressed up as sheep while underneath they are savage wolves' (Matt. 7.15; compare Acts 20. 29). Perhaps here Jesus has in mind those consistent opponents of his message, the Pharisees. It is a formidable picture of opposition – voracious wolves intent on ravaging the Church at birth. Opposition to Christ's people has taken many forms through history, sometimes violent, sometimes more subtle. But opposition is never something one can be sentimental about, as though it were a fantasy without any real force. Opponents of God's purpose in Christ are real, real as wolves.

The disciples, by contrast, are sheep. They are weak, defenceless, dependent on the protection of the Great Shepherd. We are familiar with the image of sheep gathered together in the sheepfold, guarded by the Shepherd against all attackers (John 10). But the picture here is strikingly different from that. Jesus does not speak of a flock of sheep huddled together for safety, in the manner depicted in the apocryphal book of Ecclesiasticus:

'Every animal loves its like,
and every man his neighbour.
All creatures flock together with their kind,
and men form attachments with their own sort.
What has a wolf in common with a lamb,
or a sinner with a man of piety?' (Ecclus. 13. 15–17)

Jesus says, 'I send you out . . .' For his followers there can be no true security in the fold, the ghetto, the church with its doors closed to keep the wolves at bay. Their only security is that it is their Lord who sends them, and he makes no mistake when he pushes them out among the wolves. For their very vulnerability is the key to their success.

Imagine the twelve sent out without food or money or baggage, saying to themselves: 'Suppose no one welcomes us? Suppose we can't find anywhere to stay? Suppose they refuse to listen to our message? What fools we shall look!' But the true missionary is always vulnerable. His weakness makes him depend on the God who sends him. And it makes his message credible, because it becomes plain that he has no slick techniques, no ulterior motives, nothing but the power of God. There is a strength in the weakness of uncomplicated love, like the weakness of Jesus as he approached the cross. The Church, when faced by 'wolves', has often been tempted to adopt the tactics of the wolves – to play the power game, or to rely on the security of schemes and organisations. Too easily we forget that we are sent out as sheep by one who himself 'was led like a sheep to the slaughter. . . .' (Isa. 53.7)

But there may be a further point in this sheep image. The sheep commonly symbolised Israel. In Ezek. 34, for example, the prophet denounces the leaders of Israel – whom he calls 'shepherds' – for failing to look after their flock. And there has come down to us a rabbinic conversation which went like this: 'Hadrian said to Rabbi Jehoshua, "There is something great about the sheep (Israel) that can persist among seventy wolves (the Gentile nations)." He replied, "Great is the Shepherd who delivers it and watches over it and destroys them (the wolves) before them (Israel)".' That conversation took place around AD 90, but possibly it reflects an idea current in Judaism during Jesus' lifetime. If so, Jesus would be taking a Jewish saying about Israel among the Gentiles, and applying it to his followers – the 'new Israel' or 'true Israel' – in their relationship to a potentially hostile world. In any case, it is striking that Jesus took the image of sheep, commonly applied to Israel, and used it to refer to his own little group of followers. It speaks volumes about how Jesus understood his own role as the founder of a renewed people of God, inheritors of God's Old Testament promises to Israel. 'Have no fear, little flock,' he said to his disciples on another occasion, 'for your Father has chosen to give you the Kingdom' (Luke 12.32).

The disciples must also be 'wary as serpents'. The Greek word here translated 'wary' implies prudence or shrewdness. The same word is used in the Greek Old Testment to describe the 'craftiness' of the serpent in Gen. 3.1. But here in Jesus' saying the wariness of the snake is seen as a good quality. And the snake *is* wary. It may appear idle or even lifeless as it lies on a rock in the sun. But disturb it and in a flash you will have its teethmarks in your leg. Whilst the Christian missionary is called to be vulnerable, like the sheep, he is not expected by Jesus to be naive or unaware of the real dangers which may confront him.

But that wariness must never be tinged with malice. The wariness of the snake must be balanced by the innocence of the dove. We are to cope with the wolves not by trying to be like them, but by the persuasive power of sheer goodness. Jewish rabbis sometimes used the dove as a symbol of Israel, to express the people's submissive faithfulness to God. One of their sayings goes like this: 'God says of the Israelites; "Towards me they are as sincere as doves, but towards the Gentiles they are prudent as serpents".' That, says Jesus, is the spirit in which those sent out by him are to proclaim, 'The kingdom of heaven is upon you'. (Matt. 10.8)

19

Everything is entrusted to me by my Father; and no one knows the Son but the Father, and no one knows the Father but the Son and those to whom the Son may choose to reveal him.   MATTHEW 11.27

Father and Son

Scholarly eyebrows have often been raised by this saying, because in it Jesus speaks more explicitly about his own significance and his relation to God than is normal in the first three gospels. It has been labelled a 'Johannine thunderbolt', because it looks more like the self-conscious statements of divine status found on Jesus' lips in John's Gospel (see, for example, John 5.19–26).

Jesus speaks of his Father as the origin both of what he teaches and of his authority to teach it. Interestingly, when he says 'Everything is *entrusted* to me' he uses a word which regularly denoted the passing on of a teaching or tradition. I got my teaching, he is saying, not from the fathers (as Jewish rabbis would claim) but directly from the Father, the source of all truth and authority in religion. What is here expressed in a rather veiled way was to be asserted openly by the risen Jesus to his disciples at the very end of Matthew's Gospel: 'Full authority in heaven and on earth has been committed to me . . .'. (Matt. 28.18)

'No one knows the Son but the Father, and no one knows the Father but the Son.' Probably Jesus intended this as a parable, rather than as an explicit statement that he was God's Son in a unique sense. 'Only a father and a son really know each other', he was saying. And that observation was no doubt more true of Jesus' society, where a son worked with his father and learnt his trade as he grew up, than it is in our own society with its much-publicised generation gap. Just as a father knows his son, talks to him, introduces him to the skills and the 'trade secrets' of his craft, so God has given to Jesus a unique knowledge of himself.

What does that knowledge consist of? Behind the imagery of father and son there lies Jesus' use of *Abba* in his talk with God. In his prayer in Matt. 11.25–26 and in every prayer of Jesus recorded in the gospels, apart from his cry from the cross (Mark 15.34), Jesus addressed God as 'Father'. In his account of Jesus' prayer in Gethsemane, Mark preserves the original Aramaic word which seems to underlie the Greek 'Father' in all those other prayers: 'Abba, Father, all things are possible to thee...'. (Mark 14.36) It is a family word, used by a child to his father – a word expressing intimate relationship. But its use in Gethsemane reminds us that it also conveys the idea of total, costly commitment to the father's authority: '...yet not what I will, but what thou wilt'. No Jew before Jesus had dared to address God in such intimate terms. Jesus used the terms 'Abba' for precisely the reason that Jews before him avoided it: it summed up the uniquely close relationship with God which was central to his experience and which formed the springboard for his mission.

Jesus' knowledge of God, then, was an experience of trust and security, a relationship of obedience to the God whose purposes for the world are loving. It was an awareness that the 'Lord of heaven and earth' is also the Father who cares for those who have no reason to expect his care. (see Matt. 11.25)

But let us return to the parable. 'No one knows the Father but the Son and those to whom the Son may choose to reveal him.' Only a son really knows his father, says Jesus – but that makes a son uniquely qualified to interpret his father's actions and to make him known to others. So what began as a parable about Jesus' relation to God turns out to have a message about his mission. Because God has revealed himself to a son, Jesus alone can open for others the way to real knowledge of God.

We can see that the early Christians got this message from the way in which *Abba* appears in Paul's letters. Twice, in letters to Greek-speaking readers, he refers to this Aramaic word as the authentic cry of the Christian. (Rom. 8.15; Gal. 4.6) Jesus' own use of the word must have sunk deep into the consciousness of the early Christian communities. For it expressed in a single word the fact that through his own living and dying in intimate obedience to God, he had made it possible for men and women to know God in a new way – in some sense to *share* in his own experience of God.

How shall we describe this new knowledge of God which Jesus made possible? In the first place, it is a knowledge about the character and purpose of God. If 'no one knows the Father but the Son', then we can only understand God adequately if we view him from the perspective of Jesus. As Michael Ramsey has taught us to say, 'God is Christlike, and in him is no unchristlikeness at all'. The scandalous glory of Christian faith is that everything we have to say about God has been brought into focus for us through a historical person, Jesus of Nazareth. Even though Jesus' 'parable' here contains no *explicit* claim to be 'the Son of God', he is by implication claiming to bring a unique revelation of God within reach of men and women. The validity of that claim stands or falls by whether the experience he claimed was genuine experience of God.

Secondly our knowledge of God reflects Jesus' *Abba*-relationship in being a relationship of trust and closeness to God. This relationship comes to its most typical expression in prayer. Once, when discussing with a young Christian what is involved in following Christ, I asked him whether he was managing to pray. Expecting him to express all the difficulties of praying, I was taken aback by his reply: 'Oh, it's fine,' he said, 'it's like talking to your father'. He had caught something of the reality of the *Abba*-relationship into which Jesus invites his followers.

But, thirdly, our knowledge of God is expressed in obedience to his will. Spiritual experience is not truly Christian unless it is marked by active obedience to God's will – even if that involves the agony of Gethsemane and the obedience of crucifixion. This note of obedience is underlined by the phrase 'those to whom the Son may choose to reveal him'. The mention of 'choosing' is not meant to suggest that Jesus reveals God arbitrarily to some and not to others. It means that knowledge of God comes to us by his gracious act – God is never at our disposal, like chocolates in a slot machine. On the contrary, to know him means to be at his disposal.

20

*Surely I am free to do what I like with my own money.
Why be jealous because I am kind?*

MATTHEW 20.15

Work and wages

These words are the climax of an extraordinary story.
Early one morning a landowner hired labourers to help
harvest his vines, agreeing to pay each a denarius – the
normal wage for a full day's work. At intervals during
the day he went to the market-place and hired more
labourers, promising to pay a fair wage. He even set
some workers on only an hour before sunset – perhaps
in an effort to get all the harvest in before the night
frosts of autumn spoiled it. At sunset the labourers
queued up to be paid, and those who had worked only
one hour received the same as those who had worked all
day. The complaints came quickly: 'The late-comers
have done only one hour's work, yet you have put them
on a level with us, who have sweated the whole day long
in the blazing sun!' But the owner replied, 'My friend, I
am not being unfair to you. You agreed on the usual
wage for the day, did you not? Take you pay and go
home. I choose to pay the last man the same as you.
Surely I am free to do what I like with my own money.
Why be jealous because I am kind?'

People felt strongly in those days, as they do today,
about work and unemployment, fair wages and the
need for a man to support his family. The labourers in
the story belonged to a class of free, landless men

without a skilled trade, who had to look for work each day. At harvest time work was normally plentiful, but at other times there were often large numbers of unemployed. For example, the Jewish historian Josephus tells us that after the completion of Herod's temple public works were organised in Jerusalem which provided work for eighteen thousand unemployed. The landowner in Jesus' parable is portrayed as breaking all the rules about wage levels out of compassion for the unemployed and their families. God is like that, says Jesus, and that is how things are reckoned in his kingdom.

To get the full impact of the story we need to compare it with a Jewish parable which can be found in the Jerusalem Talmud. In AD 325 an outstanding scholar, Rabbi Bun bar Hijja, died at an early age. At his funeral his former teacher Ze'era, told this story. 'There was a king who hired many labourers, and there was one labourer who understood his work exceptionally well. What did the king do? After two hours he took him by the hand and walked with him till the end of the day. When evening arrived the labourers gathered to receive their wages, and he gave each of them the same amount. The labourers grumbled and said, "We have worked the whole day, and this man has worked only two hours, and yet he has been given the same wage as we have received". The king replied: "I have done you no wrong: this labourer has done more work in two hours than you have done in the whole day".' 'In the same way', concluded Rabbi Ze'era, 'Rabbi Bun bar Hijja has achieved more in his twenty-eight years than other scholars have achieved in a long lifetime.'

It does not matter to us whether Jesus found this story current in his own day and gave a new twist to it, or whether Rabbi Ze'era picked up the story from Christians and used it for his own purposes. What matters is the way in which the comparison points up the distinctive nature of Jesus' message. The Rabbi's story says that all the labourers *deserve* the same wage because they have all done the same amount of work. Jesus' story says that if you think God works like that you completely misunderstand him. Between the two is a whole world of difference – there is the world of merit, and the world of grace.

Jesus is not proposing a new way of running wage negotiations or dealing with unemployment. He is protesting at the way in which people so often wish to limit God, requiring that he function in the same regularised and 'fair' way in which labour relations are supposed to operate. He is defending his Gospel against the legalism of the Pharisees who understand God's dealings with men in terms of work and wages, and thereby exclude from God's care the sinners, the outcasts who have no merits to clock up – the latecomers who have nothing to plead but their needs. God is gracious towards them, as he is towards those who have served him loyally over many years. The parable, then, proclaims the extravagant goodness of God in the face of the legalism which begrudges God's grace to sinner. And part of the genius of the story is that Jesus does not tell us how the workers reacted to the landowner's word about his freedom to give freely to his employees as he decides. For the reaction that matters is the reaction of those who hear the story. How do I respond to this message of God's goodness? Do I line up with those who begrudge his generosity towards those whom I regard as less worthy than myself? Or do I identify myself with those who say, 'Thank God, he does not treat us as we deserve, but loves us and accept us, unworthy as we are'?

If Jesus originally aimed the parable at his Pharisaic critics, Matthew's placing of it in his Gospel reveals its relevance to a different audience – Jesus' own followers. At the end of chapter 19 Matthew has placed the question of Peter: 'We have left everything to become your followers. What will there be for us?' And so this parable becomes Jesus' reply to the puzzled cry of the disciple who wonders whether the sacrifices he has made are worthwhile. 'In your service of Christ', it says, 'you experience, as nowhere else, the goodness of God. And if you feel resentful that God accepts the "late-comers", who have not "sweated the whole day long in the blazing sun", you must learn afresh that both you and they are recipients of the undeserved grace of God that comes to you in Christ.'

New comers to the parish.
how do we integrate them < graciously ?
                           < legally ?

21

The curse is upon you; go from my sight to the eternal fire that is ready for the devil and his angels.

MATTHEW 25.41

The great surprise

It is a common fallacy that Jesus was 'gentle, meek and mild', and that early Christians such as Paul were responsible for introducing the fiercer elements into the Christian message. In fact, we find on Jesus' lips in the gospels many warnings about God's judgement, which are more vivid in their fierceness than anything else in the New Testament, except in the Book of Revelation. If we are to take Jesus seriously, we must take his warnings seriously too.

This saying is part of the familiar 'parable' about the sheep and the goats. It is a picture of the final judgement, when the Son of Man, as King, pronounces his verdict on the lives of men and women. It involves 'all the nations' (Matt. 25.32) – that is, all people, Jew and Gentile alike, as in Matt. 24.14. Some are welcomed into God's eternal presence, while others are banished to 'eternal fire'. The judgement-scene would be familiar to Jesus' hearers, but they were in for a surprise when Jesus came to speak of the standard by which people would be judged. So the passage which is sometimes called 'the great assize' might fittingly be named 'the great surprise.'

People are condemned in the passage not for their wickedness, but for their utter failure to do good. They

are not banished from God's presence for being mur-
derers or terrorists, nor do people win a place in God's
kingdom by great heroics. It is a simple test, a test which
shows a person in his true colours. What has he done
personally for the poor, the hungry, the stranger, the
naked, the sick, the prisoner? Amongst those who fail
by this test you see the priest and the Levite who hurried
past the man on their Jericho road; the rich man who let
Lazarus die on his doorstep; the self-satisfied man who
was too busy making his barns bigger to notice those in
need.

You see too the person whom we have all heard say,
'But I never do anyone any harm'. What a miserable
standard to live by! Here is a man, created with so much
potential for good and confronted by so many needs to
be met, and all he can say is, 'I never do anyone any
harm.' The constant thrust of Jesus' challenge to the
lifestyle of his hearers was this stress on positive goodness. He expressed the so-called 'golden rule' – already
well-known in its negative form – in a new and positive
form. For instead of 'Do not do to your fellow-creature
what is hateful to you,' he urged: 'Always treat others as
you would like them to treat you.' (Matt. 7.12) He challenged the Pharisees who were not keen on sabbath healings: 'Is it permitted to do good or to do evil on the
Sabbath, to save life or to kill?' (Mark 3.4) And here in
Matt. 25 he echoed the prophetic denunciation of those
who think that God only requires them to be 'spiritual'
(see Isa. 58.6–7).

There is surprise and bewilderment in the response of
those whom the king condemns in the 'parable'. 'Lord,
when was it that we saw you hungry . . . ?' (verse 44)
We can perhaps imagine them saying at the judgement,
'But, Lord, we did not realise that it was so importtant
to respond to other people's needs. If only you had told
us that it was *you* who were confronting us in those situations'. They were not prepared to do a deed of love
just because it was there to be done, but they would do

86

it if they knew they would get something out of it.

The Son of Man, the judge of all men, is the heavenly counterpart of those who suffer on the earth. Our reaction to them *is* our reaction to him. This does not mean that we earn salvation by our good deeds: the 'surprise' theme in the passage suggests that the loving actions (or failure to do them) are the natural outworking of an underlying attitude of faith (or indifference) towards God and his will. But we must not avoid Jesus' challenge to caring action by retreating into an 'orthodoxy' which stresses salvation through faith and neglects the practical demands set out in this passage. God is bigger than our tidy systems, and he will not give up before judgement day his capacity to surprise us.

One possible way of blunting the message is to suggest that when Jesus speaks of 'anything you did for one of my brothers here' (verse 40) he is referring to people's reaction to his *followers*: their reaction to his messengers indicates their reaction to him (compare Matt.10.40). But this is unlikely, in view of the parallel with Isa. 58, and the fact that 'ill' and 'naked' look more like descriptions of general suffering than of what happens to Christ's messengers *because* they are his messengers. Also, the 'sheep' and 'goats' in the passage would know that Christ's messengers were his messengers, and so the 'surprise' theme would be inappropriate. The standard by which men are judged, then, is our reaction to those who suffer in the world.

The destiny of those who fail by this standard is 'eternal fire'. This can hardly be taken literally, since Jesus elsewhere speaks of separation from God in terms of 'darkness' (for example, Matt. 9.12, 25.30). Fire and darkness are logically incompatible if taken literally, but are both powerful pictures of condemnation by God. Nor need 'eternal fire' imply an everlasting state of conscious misery or torment. The term 'eternal' describes a destiny which is final and irreversible, but not necessarily a conscious state. The central theme in

Jesus' talk about human destiny, here and elsewhere, is his emphasis on relationship, or lack of relationship, to God. So here the king says to those on his right, 'Come' – into God's presence. And to those on his left he says, 'Go from my sight'. If some human beings are to be separated from God's presence, that is a terrible tragedy, and the precise nature of their destiny is a secondary matter on which the New Testament does not clearly pronounce.

There is one final point. This destiny is 'ready for the devil and his angels.' It was never meant for human beings at all. If men find themselves there, it is by their choice, not God's. His desired goal for them is 'the kingdom that has been ready for you since the world was made'. (verse 34)

---

22

*Anyone who wishes to be a follower of mine must leave
self behind; he must take up his cross, and come with me.*

MARK 8.34

Bearing the cross

Jesus has just warned his disciples of the sufferings
which he must undergo if he is to be loyal to the purpose
of God. The elation of Peter's recognition that Jesus is
Messiah has swiftly given way to puzzlement at why a
Messiah should have to suffer, and Peter's own blank
refusal to believe that Jesus could be destined for such
an end. Now he explains to the disciples and to all
would-be followers what is involved for *them* in following such a Messiah. Let us consider first what Jesus'
saying does *not* mean.

First, the phrase 'leave self behind' (often translated
'deny himself') does not refer to 'self-denial' in the traditional English sense. To 'give up' things – during
Lent, for example – may be healthy and may be part of
what Jesus calls for. But it is not the heart of the matter.
Jesus demands something more radical even than the
rigorous self-denial of the monk's spiritual exercises or
the pioneer missionary's readiness to abandon security
in order to make Christ known in remote places.

The second misunderstanding is one I have sometimes met among young people, who say something like
this: 'Here I am trying to find myself, struggling to dis-
cover who I am, to affirm myself as an individual
distinct from my parents. And now you are telling me

that to be a Christian I have to deny myself, to suppress my personality, to bury the real "me". If being a Christian means that my personality is shackled and my freedom to be myself and express myself is denied, then I'm not interested.' This is a totally understandable reaction, and probably more widespread than we imagine. But it arises from a false understanding of Jesus' words, as we shall see.

Thirdly, 'taking up the cross' or 'bearing the cross' does not mean accepting patiently whatever misfortunes God – or anyone else – may send upon us. There is no instance of the Greek phrase carrying that meaning, and it is a mystery how Jesus' stark words should have been diluted in this way. Of course, we should never underestimate the courage of those who bear extreme suffering in a Christian spirit. But this particular saying of Jesus does not relate specifically to their situation. It is a message for all his followers.

Jesus in fact is laying down two conditions for those who want to be his followers. First, they must 'leave self behind'. This means not 'self-denial' but 'self-surrender' – unreserved surrender of oneself to Jesus as Lord. Later, Peter 'denied Jesus' by refusing to admit that he had anything to do with him. Here Jesus calls people to 'deny themselves' by doing exactly the opposite of what Peter was to do. We are to abandon our self-centredness, our instinct for self-preservation, in obedience to the Son of Man. For one who is a follower cannot at the same time be the leader. He must take the path that the leader directs.

The second demand is to take up the cross. Readers of the gospels have sometimes expressed surprise that Jesus could have said such a thing before his own crucifixion, and it has often been suggested that the saying must have been invented by the Church after Jesus' death and resurrection. But such an explanation is hardly necessary. The cross was a sight painfully familiar to Jesus' contemporaries. When Jesus was a boy,

Varus, the Roman governor of Syria, had crushed a revolt by rebels in Palestine – including many Galileans – and had crucified two thousand of the rebels. Their dying bodies hung by the roadsides as a grim demonstration of the horror of crucifixion and the pointlessness of further revolt. Jesus' words call to mind the moment when a condemned man emerged from the judgement hall carrying the cross-piece (the horizontal bar of the cross) on his shoulder. Staggering to the place of execution, he would face the jeering of hostile crowds who lined his route through the streets. An outcast from society, he was as good as dead. Indeed, it was said among Jews: 'Anyone who strikes a man who is being led out to execution is free of punishment, for the victim counts as a dead man'.

Jesus means, then, that any follower of his must be ready for a life that is as hard as that last walk of the condemned man. He must be willing to face hostility, to be prepared even for martyrdom. But in reckoning with that possibility, he knows that he is following in the steps of his master, whose obedience led him to crucifixion. And he knows that just as Jesus was vindicated by God in resurrection, so he too can be confident of God's care through suffering and death into a new life.

That, says Jesus, is what is involved in following me. It is striking that the Greek verbs for 'leave behind' and 'take up' suggest a once-for-all action. A clear-cut decision must be made to turn from self-centredness to self-surrender under the lordship of Jesus, and to set off with Christ on the lonely road of discipleship, which may involve suffering and even martyrdom. But that clear-cut decision is the beginning of a life which *continually* involves self-giving for the sake of Christ and willingness to accept the cost of faithfulness to him. This note of continuing discipleship is struck in Luke's version of Jesus' saying: '. . . day after day he must take up his cross, and come with me' (Luke 9.23).

What does all this imply for the three 'misunderstand-ings' with which we began? It implies that any act of self-denial, any 'giving up of things', is as nothing unless it is the offering of a whole self surrendered to Christ's will. It implies that to follow Christ *is* costly, it requires the abandonment of self-centredness and self-concern. Yet that does not stunt us but liberates us to grow as persons, because we are *made* for self-giving. To 'lose ourselves' for the sake of Christ and his Gospel (Mark 8.35) is to find our true selves, because it is to live 'according to the Maker's instructions'. Finally, it implies that all whose obedience to Christ brings them into suffering are sustained through the suffering precisely because they are following the road '*with him*'.

23

I tell you this: there are some of those standing here who will not taste death before they have seen the kingdom of God already come in power.   MARK 9.1

The coming of the kingdom

This is one of a handful of sayings in the gospels where Jesus appears to put a limit on the time within which the kingdom of God will finally come. And this future coming of God's kingdom is linked with the coming again of Jesus as Son of Man at the end of history (Mark 8. 38). Obviously there is a problem here, which scholars have dealt with in a great variety of ways. Some have argued that because Jesus' prediction failed to come true, the whole New Testament scheme of expectation, with its hope of the return of Christ, is discredited. Rudolf Bultmann wrote that the New Testament expression of hope is untenable 'for the simple reason that the parousia (coming) of Christ never took place as the New Testament expected. History did not come to an end, and, as every schoolboy knows, it will continue to run its course.'

I am not sure that schoolboys are quite as knowledgeable as that. And I do not think that Bultmann's 'solution' to the problem is as self-evident as he thought. I want at least to suggest another way of approaching the text, which depends on four observations.

First, whilst Mark 9. 1 implies the *nearness* of the time when the kingdom would come, there are other sayings of Jesus which assume an *interval* between his death and his coming again. For example, there are his warnings of persecution for his followers (e.g. Mark 10. 35–40), his command to them to repeat the last supper (Luke 22. 19; 1 Cor. 11. 25), and the various parables which have 'waiting' as their theme (Luke 12. 35–40; Matt. 25). As well as this, there is Jesus' declaration of *ignorance* in Mark 13. 32 – 'But about that day or that hour no one knows, not even the angels in heaven, not even the Son; only the Father.' So unless we are prepared to argue that Jesus' teaching was confused and inconsistent, we must try to understand how he himself could have reconciled these apparently contradictory statements in his own mind.

Secondly, we know that Jesus criticised the view – which was widespread among the Pharisees – that the date of God's final triumph could be calculated by means of numerical information from the book of Daniel. A rare protest against such practices amongst the rabbis came from one of them, Rabbi Jonathan, early in the third century: 'May the bones of the end-time calculators be scattered who, when the date of the end comes without the Messiah arriving, say "He will never come at all". Rather, tarry for him as it is written, "If he delays, tarry for him".' But Jesus had already made clear his own disapproval of such attitudes in response to the Pharisees' questions, 'When will the kingdom of God come?' He said, 'You cannot tell by observation when the kingdom of God comes . . .' (Luke 17. 20) The appearance of the kingdom of God is not something which will be forshadowed by signs enabling calculation.

Thirdly, we should recognise that this enthusiasm for calculation is what happens when the poetic, visionary language of the prophet is treated with unimaginative literalism. Jesus' language is prophetic, visionary rather than chronological. Recall those lines in the hymn, 'Stand up, stand up for Jesus':

'. . . the strife will not be long;
This day the noise of battle,
The next the victor's song . . .'

When we sing it, we do not mutter furiously that it is not true, because we sang it a month ago and still we are waiting for the day of the victor's song. We recognise it as a poetic expression of the certainty that the triumph of Christ *will* one day be complete. Why, then, should we fail to recognise the same poetic flexibility in Jesus' own statements about the 'nearness' of the kingdom's coming?

Fourthly, right through the prophetic writings of the Old Testament and the New Testament, there is a tendency to express hopes of deliverance and warnings of judgement in a way which seems to suggest that the day of their fulfilment is just round the corner. Jesus' predictions that the coming of the kingdom is near fit into a familiar pattern. This pattern is there, I suggest, because in the purpose of God each crisis, each judgement, each manifestation of the saving presence of God is a partial expression within history of the ultimate triumph of God. So if Jesus said that the powerful coming of God's kingdom was less than a lifetime away, he was affirming that in his ministry the time for fulfilling the ancient prophecies had really dawned, the effects of God's rule were already making their presence felt there and then, and therefore nothing could stop the ultimate victory of God's loving purpose in Christ.

If we look closer at Mark 9. 1 we can see how this general approach makes sense of this particular text. We know from other sayings that Jesus believed the kingdom of God to be already partially present in his own ministry. For example, 'If it is by the Spirit of God that I drive out the devils, then be sure the kingdom of God has already come upon you.' (Matt. 12. 28) And, 'In fact the kingdom of God is among you.' (Luke 17.

21) And we know that Jesus expected future events such as his resurrection and the destruction of Jerusalem, which he saw as crucial events in the fulfilling of God's purposes. Here in Mark 9. 1 Jesus declares that 'some' of those listening to him – that is, the disciples as opposed to the uncommitted crowd who are looking on, Mark 8. 34 – will, before they die, recognise the powerful presence of God's rule through his action in historical events.

With hindsight we can point to events such as Jesus' resurrection, Pentecost, the growth of the Church, as examples of events where the presence of God's rule is made known. And this perspective encourages us to look at events in the world today, in the Church and in our own lives, as events which embody the presence of God's kingdom, and which foreshadow the ultimate triumph of his purposes.

24

The Spirit of the Lord is upon me
because he has anointed me;
he has sent me to announce good news
to the poor. LUKE 4.18

Nazareth manifesto

It is one of the most dramatic scenes in the New Testament. Nazareth is an unimportant place, which does not rate a mention in the Old Testament. But for a few hundred people, and for Jesus, it is home. The synagogue is full for the sabbath service. Jesus, invited to read the Scriptures, reads the passage from Isa. 61 which announces the coming of God's time of salvation. At the end of the reading he sits down (as was the custom) to teach. Every eye is fixed on him in anticipation of what the 'local boy' might say. And he begins: 'Today in your very hearing this text has come true.' (verse 21)

Let us get at the meaning of this by asking a series of questions. First, what does Jesus mean by 'Today'? He means that the longed-for time of salvation has dawned. The plan of God announced by the prophets – a plan to bring in an era of peace and liberation, justice and security in the presence of God – has reached a stage of decisive fulfilment. Jesus himself, through whom the Spirit of God is uniquely at work, is the bringer of the new era. Because he is in their midst, a new reality has entered into history. Although he does not use here the term 'kingdom of God', it is that reality of which Jesus speaks. The core of his whole message was that the 'kingdom' or 'reign' of God for which his people longed was already present – though not yet fully present – in his own ministry.

The second question is: Who are the poor? For it is to them that his message is addressed. Often in the Old Testament and Judaism 'the poor' are not simply those who experience material poverty. The term refers to those who are powerless, though usually of course it is their material poverty which makes them powerless. They are powerless as compared with others who are in a position to dominate them. But they are the ones who cast themselves on God and his mercy because they have nowhere else to go. They are empty, and therefore open to God (see Pss. 70.5; 40.17; 109.31). In Jesus' mind the poor included those who were powerless in the face of the religious establishment. There were people who stood no chance of acceptance by God because they did despised jobs – tax-collectors, prostitutes, pig-keepers, for example.

In Jewish terms there was no practical way out for such sinners. In theory, a prostitute could be made clean by repentance, purification and atonement. But that would cost money, and her ill-gotten gains could not be used for it. So she stood no chance. She was trapped in disgrace and condemnation.

For Jesus, the poor would also include the sick, the widows, the orphans, who only survived by dependence on other people's charity. There was a saying: 'Four things are compared with a dead man: the lame, the blind, the leper and the childless'. Those are the poor. The people who have no hope, unless God should do something for them.

There is, then, a flexibility in this word 'poor' as the Bible uses it. It often does refer to shortage of wordly wealth. But closely related to that is the idea of openness to God, willingness to look to him and depend on his mercy. And from this it follows that Jesus is not saying the good news is for the poor *only* and not for the rich. He says elsewhere that it is dangerous to be rich because wealth blinds you to your utter need of God (Luke 6.24; 12.13–21; 18.18–30). But if a rich man sees his need of God's love and forgiveness, and is willing to use his riches in the care of others, he too may experience God's saving power.

Thirdly we must ask, What is the good news which Jesus announces? His quotation from Isaiah continues: 'He has sent me to proclaim release for prisoners and recovery of sight for the blind, to let the broken victims go free, to proclaim the year of the Lord's favour'. Some interpreters understand this quite literally. Jesus, they say, saw his work as being to bring deliverance to those who were oppressed by unjust political and economic systems. But already in Isaiah the language is not intended literally. The prophet was speaking of people who were prisoners of hopelessness rather than to people actually in prison. And Jesus' good news for the poor is not a guarantee of instant deliverance from poverty. It is a promise that God accepts the poor if they come to him as they are, that he gives them a new beginning, a new sense of their value to him. The rest of Luke's Gospel shows us Jesus bringing to people forgiveness, new life, new relationships. It does not show us Jesus getting people such as John the Baptist out of prison. The good news is not meant literally in that sense.

And yet it would be wrong to conclude that Jesus was concerned only about 'spiritual' salvation. For although he did not guarantee economic liberation for all, he did form a community of followers in which the consequences of his forgiving and transforming were worked out. In that group were people classified by society as poor and outcast and hopeless, who embodied in their relationship to Jesus and to each other the liberation which is God's desire for all people. So they became a sign of hope, a pointer towards God's final kingdom when everything that stunts human life will be removed.

And in the Acts of the Apostles Luke shows us the early church developing its life as an embodiment of Jesus' good news for the poor, a place where wealth was shared with those in need, and barriers between rich and poor, Jew and Gentile, slave and free person were broken down.

So we have to ask, Who are the poor in our society? Who are the outcast, the dependent, the powerless? An how can Jesus' good news and God's acceptance of them be proclaimed and embodied in the life of his people?

25

No prophet is recognised in his own country.

LUKE 4.24

Prophet and loss

What looked at first like a 'local boy makes good' story turns out to be nothing of the kind. Jesus announced the coming of God's reign, and the whole synagogue was astir with excitement at the promise of his blessings. But quickly things turned nasty. 'Isn't this Joseph's son?', they say. 'Who does he think he is? He hasn't been trained to say this sort of thing. His training is only in sawing and planing and hammering. And here he is hammering us with this message about the Spirit of the Lord being upon him. We are proud when a local boy becomes a famous craftsman or a footballer or even a well-known rabbi. It puts us on the map. But the boy-next-door become Messiah? That's intolerable.'

Jesus' response shows up the world of difference between their understanding and his understanding of God's purposes, as we shall see. 'No doubt you will quote the proverb to me, "Physician, heal yourself!", and say, "We have heard of all your doings at Capernaum; do the same here in your own home town." I tell you this', he went on: 'no prophet is recognised in his own country.' (Luke 4.23–24) And he reminded them how, despite the needs on their own doorstep, the prophets Elijah and Elisha had brought God's help to foreigners. Elijah had enabled a widow in Sarepta (in what is now Lebanon) to survive a drought and had re-

101

stored her dying son. Elisha had healed the leprosy of Naaman, a Syrian army commander.

That was more than they could take. In fury they jostled him out of the town, meaning to push him headlong over the nearby cliff. Jesus fixed his gaze on them, averted their anger and walked calmly through the mob to safety. His time had not yet come. But there was to be another city, where Jesus would be rejected, and another hill, where he would meet his death . . .

Why did the audience react so violently? Clearly, their feelings ran deep. They were annoyed, perhaps, that Jesus had worked miracles at Capernaum rather than bringing relief to Nazareth's sufferers first. And they were demanding that Jesus should perform miraculous signs to prove the truth of his astounding claims. Both those thoughts seem to lie behind Jesus' reference to the proverb, 'Physician, heal yourself!' (verse 23). It implies both 'Charity begins at home', and 'Do a miracle for us so that we can be sure you speak God's truth'.

To this pique is added a fierce disagreement about God and his purposes. What right has Jesus to declare that God accepts the outcasts of society? And Gentiles! Has not God promised to bring deliverance to his people and to work vengeance on the Gentiles who do not acknowledge him and cause nothing but suffering for his chosen people? Did not Isaiah speak of 'the year of the Lord's favour and the day of vengeance of our God'? (Isa. 61.2) And yet Jesus in his reading of that passage has stopped short of announcing God's vengeance on the Gentiles. (Luke 4.19) He is overthrowing our faith!

Exactly. For Jews of Jesus' time the supreme religious duty was to keep clear of sinners. And the popular assumptions about Gentiles were expressed like this: 'No Gentile will have a part in the world to come.' Or this: 'Whoever spills the blood of one of the godless is like one who offers sacrifice.' Jesus' audience

in Nazareth expected to have their assumptions confirmed. Like us when we watch *Starsky and Hutch* they
knew that the good guys always win through and the bad
guys get brought to justice. And they were outraged
when Jesus challenged the assumption on which they
based their social and religious security.

'No prophet is recognised in his own country'. It is not
simply that we do not like the boy-next-door telling us
how to behave, though that is true. We are all inclined
to be more impressed by someone who comes from afar
than by someone with whom we have grown up. More
seriously, prophets tend to be rather close to the mind
of God, and that requires them often to say uncomfortable things to us. So there is a long tradition of prophets
being uncomfortable for their own people – Elijah,
Jeremiah, John the Baptist, for example. And the mind
of God now, already foreshadowed in the lives of Elijah
and Elisha, was to bring his blessing to Gentiles as well
as to Jews. God has no favourites. Those who think they
are first will find themselves last. And Luke in his
Gospel shows us a Jesus who is constantly reaching out
to the lost, the downtrodden, the despised – a Jesus who
announces after his resurrection that 'in his name repentance bringing the forgiveness of sins is to be proclaimed
to all nations'. (Luke 24.47)

You can have your Messiah and his blessings, says
Jesus, as long as you are willing for others to have him
too. But you cannot have the blessings of God's reign if
you expect him to make your nation to prosper at the
expense of others – whether your nationalism is Jewish,
British, American or of any other sort. It is easy for us
to think how narrow-minded the people of Nazareth
were, and to indulge in the same smug nationalism as
we condemn in them. How, I wonder, do they react
today in the synagogue at Nazareth when the story is
read of how Naaman the Syrian was healed by an
'Israeli' prophet? And how do they react at the church
by the crossroads when finance is short and there is a

crying need for community work amongst unemployed black young people? If Jesus challenged the comfortable assumptions and value-systems of his contemporaries, he has equally disturbing questions to raise against the instincts for nationalism and self-preservation in God's people today. What he said to the people of Nazareth he says to everyone: You can have God's Messiah, and all his blessings – if you will recognise him as Messiah for all peoples.

26

Go and tell that fox, 'Listen: today and tomorrow I shall be casting out devils and working cures; on the third day I reach my goal.'　　　　　　　LUKE 13.32

Message for a fox

Herod Antipas, son of Herod the Great, was ruler of Galilee and Perea (which was east of the River Jordan) during Jesus' ministry. He had already distinguished himself by having John the Baptist beheaded (Mark 6.17–29). Herod did not like disturbance in his realm, not did he like people meddling with his morals. That had led to John's downfall. And now Jesus was under threat because he too was causing a stir amongst the people. Jesus got the news from a group of Pharisees. 'You should leave this place and go on your way', they urged; 'Herod is out to kill you'. (Luke 13.31) Were these Pharisees friendly towards Jesus, and doing him a favour by warning him what was afoot? Or were they hostile, using this story of Herod's threat as a way of pushing Jesus out of their district? Probably they were friendly. Jesus certainly took their warning at face value. He did not accuse them of hypocrisy, as he could well have done if he thought there was an ulterior motive in their message. If I am right about this, then we have here a reminder that Pharisees were not uniformly hostile to Jesus. There were men like Nicodemus (John 3.1; 19.39), and these Pharisees in Galilee.

Jesus' reply raises some significant questions. 'Go and tell that fox . . .', he begins. Not the best way to maintain good relations with the powers that be, you would imagine. Not exactly what you would expect from 'Gentle Jesus, meek and mild'. In the Old Testament the fox (or jackel – in Greek and Hebrew the two animals are not clearly distinguished) symbolised destructiveness. Ezekiel said the false prophets of Israel were like foxes, bringing the nation to its ruin (Ezek. 13.4). The Greeks had many fables about foxes made famous by Aesop. In his fables the fox is depicted as crafty. And in several fables the fox is contrasted with the lion: the fox is inferior in strength but uses his craftiness – often in an unprincipled way – to outwit other animals and avoid being eaten by the lion. And similar ideas may be found in the Judaism of Jesus' day or a little later. One rabbi said it was better to be the tail of a lion than the head of a fox.

So by calling Herod a fox Jesus was implying that Herod was a scheming, unprincipled, second-rate ruler, causing nothing but disaster for his subjects. Now, how do we reconcile that attitude with Jesus' command to 'love your enemies and pray for your persecutors'? (Matt. 5.44) Or with his total silence when questioned by Herod at his trial? (Luke 23.6–12) Does not this denunciation of Herod show Jesus as one who fanned the flames of hatred and division between oppressor and oppressed? Does his attitude justify the actions of those among his followers who believe that the only way to change society for the better is to get rid of corrupt rulers by violent revolution?

Certainly we must acknowledge the full force of Jesus' condemnation of Herod. Like Nathan confronting David (2 Sam. 12), or Elijah denouncing Arab (1 Kgs 18), he overflows with divine anger at powerful people who abuse their power to squash the defenceless, the poor, or the saint who disturbs their conscience. And so it must be. Compassion for 'little ones' who are tripped up and led away from the truth must be accompanied by anger with those who cause them to trip. (Matt. 18.6–7) To suggest otherwise is sheer romanticism. Love for 'the enemy' sometimes has to bear the responsibility of pointing out the error, the wickedness of 'the enemy's' actions. That is a painful process. Painful for 'the enemy' if he is in fact to respond to the message of judgement. Painful for the prophet who takes the risk of delivering the message. It took John the Baptist and Jesus to their deaths. If Jesus was *against* Herod and other abusers of influence in Palestine, that is because he was *for* people and *for* society. Love and truthful confrontation are not mutually exclusive.

Then came the message which Jesus wanted Herod to hear: 'Today and tomorrow I shall be casting out devils and working cures; on the third day I reach my goal.' In other words, Jesus refused to be bullied by Herod's threats of murder. He would not be diverted from his God-given task by a second-rate politician. The time for dying would come – Jesus' comment in verse 33 makes that plain: 'I must be on my way today and tomorrow and the next day, because it is unthinkable for a prophet to meet his death anywhere but in Jerusalem.'

We see in Jesus' reply to Herod the significance which he himself gave to his healings and exorcisms. They were not the only concerns of his ministry, but they were important enough to be highlighted here in his own description of what his ministry was about. The triumph over evil forces, the restoration of broken personalities and of sick bodies were – and are – signs that in Jesus the loving reign of God is present among men and women. Those who are suspicious of miracle stories in the gospels, and wish to attribute them to the imagination of the early church and the gospel-writers, must also reckon with Jesus' own testimony to his miracles, which is much harder to dismiss as unauthentic.

Another interesting feature of Jesus' saying is his reference to 'the third day'. The term is more familiar to us in connection with his resurrection, but here it refers to the completion of a short, though uncertain, period of time. Semitic languages such as Hebrew and Aramaic have no word for 'some' or 'a few'. So they use numbers such as 'two' and 'three' to indicate a short but unspecified period (e.g., Hos, 6.2: 'after two days he will revive us, on the third day he will restore us'). So here Jesus is telling Herod that he will continue his ministry for God's appointed time, and this ministry will reach its decisive point in his 'reaching his goal'. He is a man of destiny, whose obedience to the plan of God will be crowned with death at Jerusalem.

27

It was this man, I tell you, and not the other, who went home acquitted of his sins.   LUKE 18.14

The prayer which God hears

Two men slipped into church to pray. One was a vicar, the other a tramp with convictions for rape and petty thieving to his name. The vicar's prayer was full of thanksgiving and praise to God. 'Thank you', he began, 'for counting me fit to be a disciple of yours. Thank you for making me such a special person, different from other people who are so materialistic and selfish. Thank you that I'm not like that tramp, who never does anything useful and is a plague to the neighbourhood.' The tramp found a dark corner and stared at the floor. 'God,' he blurted out, 'I'm sorry. I've lived a rotten life. Have pity on me.'

That is how the story needs to be told today if we are to get any inkling of how shocking was Jesus' comment on his story about the Pharisee and the tax-collector: 'It was this man – the tax-collector – and not the other, who went home acquitted for his sins.' Our problem is that we know too much. We know that the Pharisees are the bad guys in the gospel records. As soon as this story begins, we know that the Pharisee is going to be condemned for his smugness. And we know that Jesus had a soft spot for tax-collectors, so we are not too surprised when we hear that Jesus declares this tax-collector forgiven. Thus the story confirms our assumptions – our assumptions that pharisaism is a bad thing, and that *we* are not pharisees.

It must have been very different when Jesus first told the parable, for the whole point of it was to challenge the assumptions of his contemporaries about the way God deals with men and women. To the people of Jesus' day, the Pharisee was a respected religious leader. If anyone was close to God, the Pharisee was. He had status with God, and with men. Most importantly, his prayer in the parable was not unusual. It was a typical Pharisaic prayer, familiar to Jesus' hearers. It was the way a good man was *supposed* to pray. Here is a Pharisee's prayer which has come down to us from the first century:

'I thank you, O Lord, my God, that you have given me my lot with those who sit in the seat of learning, and not with those who sit at the street-corners; for I am early to work, and they are early to work; I am early to work on the words of the Law, and they are early to work on things of no moment. I weary myself, and they weary themselves; I weary myself and profit thereby, and they weary themselves to no profit. I run and they run; I run towards the life of the Age to Come, and they run towards the pit of destruction.'

So the prayer which Jesus puts on the Pharisee's lips is a prayer taken from real life. This Pharisee is a normal, respected, spiritual man, whose prayer is full of thanksgiving. He is grateful that God preserves him from being like other men, who flout God and his will. He is pleased to honour God by going far beyond the requirements of the Jewish law. He fasts not once a year but twice a week. He pays tithes (ten per cent) of all that he buys – just in case his purchases of corn, wine and oil have not already been tithed by their producers.

The tax-collector, by contrast, hides in a corner and does not even adopt the normal attitude of prayer.

Rather than raise his eyes and hands to heaven, he beats his breast in utter despair. He is trapped by his years of involvement in fraud. He cannot get out of this situation because he has no way of knowing everyone whom he has cheated, so he can never put right the wrongs he has done. He can only cry for mercy.

And he finds it. In contrast to the Pharisee, says Jesus, the tax-collector 'went home acquitted of his sins'. The first hearers of this verdict must have been stunned, confused, maybe speechless with anger. But perhaps there were some too who found new hope, because they saw in the tax-collector a reflection of themselves. But *why* should he go home forgiven while the Pharisee carried with him his catalogue of unforgiven achievements? What wrong had the Pharisee done? What sign had the tax-collector given that he was prepared to restore his fraudulent gains to their owners?

Jesus' answer to the question 'why?' is implied in the tax-collector's prayer. For it echoes Psalm 51: 'Have mercy on me, O God . . .' God, says Jesus, is the God depicted in Psalm 51, one who welcomes the despairing and gives hope to those who cast themselves on his mercy.

'My sacrifice, O God, is a broken spirit;
a wounded heart, O God, thou wilt not despise.'
(Ps. 51.17)

And Jesus' point is summed up in a description of two kinds of religion: 'Everyone who exalts himself will be humbled' (that is, will have his values and assumptions overturned by God); 'and whoever humbles himself will be exalted'. (Luke 18.14)

So we learn something about ourselves, and about God. About ourselves, we see how easy it is to build our approach to God on the fantasy that he approves of us because of our moral achievements or religious convictions. Paul, who before his conversion regarded himself as 'in legal rectitude, faultless' (Philippians 3.6), came to see the folly of that. The only genuine approach to God is that which says, in effect: 'We do not presume to come to this your table, merciful Lord, trusting in our own righteousness, but in your manifold and great mercies . . .' And it will not do even to say 'I thank thee, O God, that I am not like that Pharisee, hypocritical . . .' For that is only another way of making the Pharisee's mistake.

As for God, we see that he welcomes men and women without preconditions and with boundless generosity. W. B. Yeats wrote in his autobiography: 'Can one reach God by toil? He gives himself to the pure in heart. He asks nothing but attention.' The most 'lost' of men is nearer to God than the man who is sure of his own goodness.

28

'Look, Lord,' they said, 'we have two swords here.'
'Enough, enough!' he replied.   LUKE 22.38

Jesus and violence

There must have been times when Jesus' disciples were
exasperated by what Jeus said. His teaching must have
seemed sometimes too idealistic, sometimes too out-
rageously new. There were certainly times when Jesus
himself was exasperated by their slowness to grasp his
message. They seemed totally incapable of tuning in to
his wavelength. This saying at the Last Supper is a case
in point.

Now it is true that some readers of the story have
taken these words of Jesus at face value. Immediately
before (verse 35), Jesus had urged any of the twelve
who had no sword to sell his cloak to buy one. And
when they produced two swords, Jesus replied, 'It is
enough'. In other words, a couple of swords will be
enough to stage an effective resistance against those
who will try to arrest him. Add to this the opening statement of the prosecution at his trial before Pilate – 'We
found this man subverting our nation, opposing the
payment of taxes to Caesar, and claiming to be Messiah,
a king'. (Luke 23.2) Then there was the inscription
nailed on to his cross, stating the charge on which he
was condemned: 'The king of the Jews'. (Mark 15.26)
Note also that one of Jesus' disciples was Simon the
Zealot, and you have the makings of a plausible argument for the view that Jesus was a political revolution-

ary, prepared to adopt the tactics of the Zealot guerilla movement to deliver Palestine from Roman oppression. And you can find a slogan for this revolutionary movement in Jesus' saying, in Matt. 10.34, 'You must not think that I have come to bring peace to the earth; I have not come to bring peace, but a sword'.

However, such an argument is totally implausible, once you set alongside it certain other evidence from the gospels. First, there is not a trace of nationalism in Jesus' preaching about God's kingdom. On the contrary, he predicted the destruction of Jerusalem and its temple (Mark 13), and declared God's concern for people of all races – including a Roman centurion. (Luke 7.1–10) He knew well enough about Roman brutality but refused to use this knowledge to fan the flames of anti-Roman feelings, as we see in Luke 13.1–5: 'There were some people present who told him about the Galileans whose blood Pilate had mixed with their sacrifices. He answered them: "Do you imagine that, because these Galileans suffered this fate, they must have been greater sinners than anyone else in Galilee? I tell you they were not; but unless you repent, you will all of you come to the same end".' News which might have provoked a tirade against Roman atrocities in fact produced a call to repentance.

Secondly, Jesus saw the coming of God's kingdom in his healings and exorcisms, rather than in any acts of armed force.

Thirdly, the temptation stories (Matt. 4.1–10; Luke 4.1–12) show that for Jesus the temptation to win the world's allegiance by political and military means was a real temptation – which he resisted. Jesus saw himself as called to be not a man of war but a suffering servant, offering up his life as 'a ransom for many'. (Mark 10.45)

Fourthly, Jesus taught his disciples to love their enemies, even to the extent of travelling an extra mile when press-ganged by a Roman soldier or government agent to carry his baggage. (Matt. 5.38–48)

Fifthly, if Jesus had really advocated revolutionary violence, it would be very odd that, after his death, the Romans made no attempt to stop the new Christian community spreading in Palestine. And if there had been armed resistance in Gethsemane, the authorities would not have allowed the disciples to escape so easily.

So we return to our passage, and Jesus' conversation in the upper room. When the disciples inform him that they have two swords, his reply 'It is enough'must not be taken literally, as though it were a grateful acceptance of their contribution. It is a frustrated conclusion to a conversation in which the disciples have already shown how little still they understand Jesus and his way. On the very eve of his greatest crisis they have been arguing vigorously which of them is the greatest. (Luke 22.24–27) And Peter has been protesting confidently that trials and even the threat of martyrdom will be no problem for him. (Luke 22.31–34)

Jesus' command to the disciples to buy swords (verse 36) must be a grimly ironical reference to the intensity of the opposition which they are about to face. They must be ready for extreme hardship and self-sacrifice, if they are to be true followers of their master. But, dull as ever, they understand his command literally. Jesus, exasperated, breaks off the conversation. 'Enough of that', he says. Soon afterwards, in the darkness of Gethsemane, a disciple would offer vain resistance in cutting off the ear of the high priest's servant with his sword. And Jesus would demonstrate *his* attitude by restoring the ear to health. (Luke 22.49–51)

Why did Jesus take this stand against the use of violence? Certainly not because he cherished the status quo – his unpopularity with the Jewish authorities, his opposition to vested interests, his warnings about the love of power, are enough to show that. He opposed the Zealot's tactics because he was more, not less, revolutionary than they were. They wanted to restore the kingdom of Israel. He wanted to create a renewed

Israel, open to all nations. They wanted to win political freedom. He saw that men needed a larger freedom which could only be won through his own self-giving, his acceptance of suffering in costly obedience to the plan of God.

Jesus' rejection of violence for his own mission does not, perhaps, wholly rule out the use of force by some Christians in some situations. But it certainly means that the use of violence can never be an easy option or a first resort. And Jesus' total attitude forbids the Christian to use his abhorrence of violence as an excuse for refusing to get involved in struggles for social justice and human liberation.

29

You are my friends, if you do what I command you.
JOHN 15.14

Friends of Jesus

I have often puzzled over the way in which Jesus, according to John's Gospel, links together love and obedience. In our minds the two ideas are not natural companions. We would not expect to win popularity with people by saying, 'If you do what I tell you, you can be my friend.' Indeed, we tell our children that if they take that attitude they will not have any friends. To understand what Jesus means we shall have to look at the wider context in which his saying is placed.

The paradox of love and obedience is already there in verses 9 and 10: 'As the Father has loved me, so I have loved you. Dwell in my love. If you heed my commands, you will dwell in my love, as I have heeded my Father's commands and dwell in his love.' This gives the first clue as to how Jesus' words are to be understood. There is a chain of thought: Father – Son – believer. This reminds us that the connection between love and obedience was there in Jesus' own life and relationship with God. It was summed up in his speaking to God as *Abba* (Mark 14.36), a family term which expressed both deep intimacy and total obedience. And John's Gospel presents us with a consistent picture of Jesus living in total obedience to the Father's directions. 'It is meat and drink for me to do the will of him who sent me'. (John 4.34) 'I always do what is acceptable to him'. (John 8.29) Yet it is precisely this obedience and depen-

117

dence on the Father that enables him to say, 'My Father
and I are one'. (John 10.30)

In the relationship of Son to Father, love and obedience are mutually dependent. Love arises out of obedience, and obedience arises out of love. And that
relationship, says Jesus, is to be reflected in the believer's relationship to him. Paradoxical though it may
seem, it is the general experience of Christians that
increased love for Jesus leads to a greater desire to do
his will, and deeper obedience leads to an increase of
love. This is because Jesus is recognised as lord rather
than as an equal. He is one whose love has done things
for us before we were even aware of him. Hence every
expression of his love towards us comes as an unexpected discovery, a cause of joy. This note of unexpected
discovery comes through in verses 14–15: 'You are my
beloved' ('friends' is too weak a translation), 'if you do
what I command you. I call you servants no longer; a
servant does not know what his master is about. I have
called you my beloved, because I have disclosed to you
everything that I heard from my Father.' Presumably
Jesus does not mean here that his disciples cease to be
servants. But they cease to be *merely* servants. A
servant simply carries out orders, without knowing how
they fit into the master's plan. Beloved ones still carry
out orders, but they know what the master is aiming at,
and so their obedience is lifted into the realm of love.

A further question we must ask is this: does not Jesus
seem to be saying that experience of his love is a kind of
reward for being obedient? No, because the obedience
of the believer flows naturally from being loved by
Jesus. The love of Jesus, or of God, is always there first,
as we saw in the chain linking Father, Son and believer
in verses 9 and 10. And it is underlined in what follows:
'You did not choose me: I chose you. . . .' (verse 16) So
the love of God in Christ is the force behind us. And we
express our love in return by obedience to Jesus' commands. But what commands?

Jesus' answer is in verse 12: 'This is my commandment: love one another, as I have loved you.' You will
search John's Gospel in vain to find any commandments
more specific than this. For Christian discipleship is relationship to a person, not adherence to a set of rules.
Jesus did not give a new law which could be used like a
cookery book to look up what one must do. He called
people to a new life which involves asking time and
again what form of obedience to him must take today.

Often we go wrong, we leave behind the way of love,
and it is almost stretching the meaning of words to say
we are still 'dwelling in him'. Yet he deals with us, not
by giving us a list of rules, but by setting us off once
again on the painful, maturing process of learning what
it means to love him and to live by his commandment to
love.

But why a *command* to love? Can love be command-
ed? There are two things to say about this. First, God is
realistic about our need to be exhorted and to make
efforts in response to him. Just as Judaism speaks of a
command to hope, so Jesus has a command to love.
Secondly, love is mainly – if not entirely – a matter of
the will, and therefore can be a proper subject for
exhortation.

But the fundamental thing about love as it is here
described is that it is love 'as I have loved you'. (verse
12) Jesus is the source of love – the love of the Father for
the Son is 'passed on' from the Son to those who 'dwell
in him'. (verse 10) The command to love always
includes the gift of the power to love, because it starts
from God. And Jesus shows how love is to be expressed
– by self-giving action: 'There is no greater love than
this, that a man should lay down his life for those whom
he loves'. (verse 13) Love is not mainly a mystical relationship to Jesus, but a passing on of his caring to
others.

The demands of love are infinite – there is always
more loving to do. Therefore there is always room for

119

repentance and progress. We can never settle down, thinking we have 'done our duty'. But the demands of love derive from God whose love is infinite. Therefore we always stand under his grace, and his resources of love never run dry.

30

My kingdom does not belong to this world . . .
My kingly authority comes from elsewhere.

JOHN 18.36

A kingdom not of this world

Jesus' words to Pilate have caused much misunderstanding. In particular, they have often been used to justify the view that the Church has no business meddling in politics. For they appear to drive a sharp wedge between the political and spiritual realms. When a group of bishops tried to bring government, mineowners and miners together to find a solution to the disastrous miners' strike of 1926, the Prime Minister, Mr Baldwin, asked how the bishops would like it if he referred to the Iron and Steel Federation the revision of the Athanasian Creed. He did not actually quote our text, but there have been many before and after him who, on the basis of Jesus' saying, have confined the gospel to a narrow 'spiritual' sphere, and have left the world to get on with its own affairs in its own way.

One who did cite Jesus' words was Benjamin Hoadly, who in the early eighteenth century was bishop of four dioceses in turn, although he was too busily engaged in politics to pay them more than occasional visits. In a famous sermon of 1717 he argued that since Christ had said his kingdom was not of this world, the Church was invisible too. And since it was invisible, it had no right to exercise power over worldly matters of any kind.

This attitude may be better than the Church's

attempts in the past to advance God's kingdom by the use of political and military force. The misguided adventurism of the Crusades has taken centuries to live down, and in Islamic countries it remains today a serious obstacle to Christian witness. Yet, to use Jesus' words as a catch-phrase to keep the Church out of politics is to abuse them. Let us set the saying in its context.

The Jewish authorities had found Jesus guilty of claiming to be Messiah and Son of God. That was quite enough to damn him in their eyes. But only the Roman governor had authority to put a man to death. So they brought Jesus to Pilate, reporting that he was subversive, claiming to be Messiah or king, and therefore provoking revolt. (see Luke 22.66–23.5) The governor could not fail to take seriously such a political charge. It was more than his own skin was worth to let this prisoner loose in Judea, if he did indeed claim to be a king.

So he examined Jesus privately. 'Are you the king of the Jews?', he enquired. He hardly looked like a threat to the emperor, but the question had to be asked. 'That is the charge they are laying against you, so what have you got to say for yourself?' Jesus' reply confirmed Pilate's suspicion that he was no stereotyped revolutionary: 'My kingdom does not belong to this world. If it did, my followers would be fighting to save me from arrest by the Jews. My kingly authority comes from elsewhere.' Recognising that Jesus was no revolutionary threat, Pilate could relax a little. 'So you are a king, are you?', he continued. '"King" is your word. My task is to bear witness to the truth. For this I was born; for this I came into the world, and all who are not deaf to truth listen to my voice'. (John 18.37) Jesus did not deny that it was appropriate to call him king, but insisted that his kingship was in a higher realm than Pilate could comprehend.

Thus, having relaxed because Jesus was no threat to his position, he was made uncomfortable again by this mysterious talk about truth. From that moment on the trial was not about whether Jesus was innocent – 'I find no case against him', declared Pilate. (verse 38) The trial was now about whether Pilate would respond to truth, or whether he would suppress truth to save his own reputation by allowing an innocent man to die. With heavy irony, John tells how Pilate was persuaded to release not Jesus but Barabbas – who *was* a revolutionary – and how the Jews sealed Jesus' fate by claiming, 'We have no king but Caesar'. (John 18.40; 19.15) They regarded Jesus as such a threat, that they were prepared to deny their allegiance to God as the only true king.

What, then, was Jesus saying about his kingship? In saying that his kingdom did not belong to this world, he meant that it does not *derive* from this world, it is different from the kingship which rules by military power. His authority derives from God, and it consists in his bearing witness to truth – that is, to the eternal and overwhelming reality of God which in Jesus has made its presence felt among men and women. The subjects of this kingdom are those who are open to this truth and show personal allegiance to Jesus, the king, by 'listening to his voice'.

Now this does not mean that Jesus' kingdom has no concern with political kingdoms; for his kingship derives from a *higher* authority who is not merely Lord in the spiritual realm, but Lord over all creation. As Jesus reminded Pilate later: 'You would have no authority at all over me if it had not been granted you from above'. (John 19.11) And throughout his ministry we see Jesus not 'playing politics', yet acting and speaking in ways which carry clear political implications. He denounced Herod Antipas as a 'fox' (Luke 13.32); he condemned rulers who were oppressive while claiming to be benefactors. (Luke 22.24–27) By forming tax-collectors, zealots, the poor, into a new society, by healing on the Sabbath, by opposing the attitudes of Pharisees and Sadducees, he threatened to undermine the social, religious and political structure of the nation.

The Gospel is not politics, but there is a politics of the Gospel. True Christianity offers more than an inner spiritual experience. It proclaims the lordship of Christ over the whole of life, including the world of social need and political action. That is what F. D. Maurice was stressing when he lamented: 'We have been dosing our people with religion when what they need is not that but the living God.'

31

*Because you have seen me you have found faith. Happy
are they who never saw me and yet have found faith.*

JOHN 20.29

Believing is seeing

'Seeing is believing', we say. In this saying the risen
Christ puts a question mark against that viewpoint, and
opens a window of hope for all who were not present in
his own day to see him.

The story is familiar. Thomas had already shown
himself to be a loyal but dull and pessimistic disciple
(John 11.16; 14.5). Now, having been absent when
Jesus first appeared after his death to the disciples, he
refused to believe their story. 'Unless I can see, I will
never believe.' A week later Jesus appeared to Thomas
and the other disciples, prompting from the doubter the
confession of faith which comes as the climax of the
whole gospel story: 'My Lord and my God!'

Jesus gently rebuked Thomas for refusing to believe
the other disciples, and for being too concerned instead
to probe into the miraculous nature of his risen body.
Yet he did not despise Thomas' doubt, for out of it came
that great confession of faith – like the faith of
Dostoevsky who said, 'My hosanna has come out of the
crucible of doubt.' Thomas is in fact the fourth example
in this chapter of John's Gospel of one who 'saw and believed'. The beloved disciple looked inside the empty
tomb, saw and believed. Mary Magdalene saw the risen
Lord, and believed when he spoke her name. The other

disciples saw him and believed. And now Thomas.

But once faith has risen in him, immediately the focus of attention changes. The commentator Raymond Brown compares it with the situation in a theatre. Right through his Gospel, while the gospel-writer has been presenting on stage a drama of early first-century Palestine, he has had in mind the audience sitting in the darkened theatre – the readers of his Gospel who silently watch what Jesus on stage is saying and doing. As in any drama, the central character addresses the audience only indirectly through addressing the disciples on stage, while the audience identify with the reactions of the disciples. Now suddenly, at the climax of the drama, the lights in the theatre are turned on, and Jesus addresses the audience directly, making clear that his ultimate concern is with them.

'Happy are they who never saw me and yet have found faith.' The readers of the Gospel, and all who believe in Jesus despite being separated in time and space from the events of his earthly ministry, are equal in God's sight with those who were present with him then.

Why are they pronounced 'happy' for not having seen Jesus? Is it not a great disadvantage to have been born too late to see Jesus in the flesh? Are we not condemned to peering through the mists of time in order to catch a meagre glimpse of him? Surely if we had been there to see for ourselves we could have been so much more confident in our faith? But would we? John's Gospel presents us with numerous examples of people who 'see', and yet remain blind to the truth.

There were those who saw his miracles and thus came to have a merely superficial faith in him. (John 2.23–25; 4.48) They did not have the real faith which consists in spiritual perception of the significance of Jesus, and personal commitment to him. Then there were those whose preconceived ideas made them hostile rather than believing. When Jesus brought sight to a blind man one

Sabbath, the religious authorities could see this only as law-breaking and not as a work of God. And when Jesus told them that the very purpose of his ministry was 'to give sight to the sightless and to make blind those who see', they asked, 'Do you mean that we are blind?' And Jesus answered darkly, 'If you were blind you would not be guilty, but because you say 'We see', your guilt remains? (John 9.39–41)

There were also those who missed the significance of Jesus because they looked for truth in the wrong place. Even the scriptures, when studied without thought of Jesus, are a dead end. 'You study the scriptures diligently, supposing that in them you have eternal life; yet, although their testimony points to me, you refuse to come to me for that life! (John 5.39–40) Malcolm Muggeridge has a wry passage where he comments how consistently the news media manage to miss the most important thing. 'In moments of humility, I realise that if I had been correspondent in the Holy Land at the time of our Lord's ministry, I should almost certainly have spent my time knocking about with the entourage of Pontius Pilate, finding out what the Sanhedrin was up to, and lurking around Herod's court with the hope of signing up Salome to write her memoirs exclusively.'

That is the point. People have all kinds of reasons for failing to believe in Jesus, and those reasons were just as evident among people who witnessed his ministry as amongst those who live in later times. But there were also some who did see and believed. There were the people in Samaria, who took notice of a woman's witness, and so became able to say to her: 'It is no longer because of what you said that we believe, for we have heard him ourselves: and we know that this is in truth the Saviour of the world'. (John 4.42) There was the blind man, who on receiving his physical sight from Jesus became a believer. (John 9.25, 35–38) There were the disciples, and supremely the 'beloved disciple' on whose testimony the Fourth Gospel is based. (John

19.35; 21.24)

For the whole purpose of this Gospel is to present to those who have not seen Jesus in the flesh the evidence of first hand witness which can lead them to faith in him whom they have not seen. The evidence has been presented 'in order that you may hold the faith that Jesus is the Christ, the Son of God, and that through this faith you may possess life by his name'. (John 20.31) 'Seeing is believing,' we often say. 'No', says the risen Lord. 'Believing is the way to seeing and knowing.'